D1302694

SAMUEL PEPYS

SAMUEL PEPYS

BY

ARTHUR PONSONBY

 BOOKS FOR LIBRARIES PRESS

FREEPORT, NEW YORK

First Published 1928
Reprinted 1971

INTERNATIONAL STANDARD BOOK NUMBER:
0-8369-5855-1

LIBRARY OF CONGRESS CATALOG CARD NUMBER:
71-160987

PRINTED IN THE UNITED STATES OF AMERICA

TO

THE MASTER

AND

FELLOWS

OF

MAGDALENE COLLEGE, CAMBRIDGE

ON

THE FIVE HUNDREDTH ANNIVERSARY OF
THE FOUNDATION OF THE COLLEGE

1928

CONTENTS

CHAPTER VII

CHAPTER VIII

CHAPTER IX

INTRODUCTION

EVERY living person makes some impression on his contemporaries. When he dies the impression remains until his contemporaries die. Then it fades unless it has been sufficiently deep for some of it to be handed on to the next generation, and prolonged by report for a few years more. A small minority of people achieve sufficient distinction in their lives to have books written about them in which the impression they made on their contemporaries is amplified by notes, correspondence, and sometimes a diary. A few of them may get their paragraph, column, or pages in the *Dictionary of National Biography*, and thus their portraits, great or small, sketchy or detailed, are handed down, and can be consulted for all time even though only a few may become subjects of our historical education. So it is that everyone has one portrait, the ephemeral portrait. A small minority have a second portrait, fuller and more permanent.

The case of Samuel Pepys, however, is exceptional because there are three distinct portraits. The first is the impression he made on his contemporaries. The second is the memory left of him after his death in the long period from 1703 to the year 1825. And the third portrait is the marvellous detailed and finished picture

of the man which began to emerge when the Diary
was first published in 1825 and was completed after
the five-volume edition of the Diary was published in
1848, or perhaps we ought to say after the eight-volume
edition was completed in 1899. It was as if unsuspected
and undreamed-of scenes and details were discovered
on a canvas of little account obscured and darkened by
the passage of time.

Since the appearance of this astonishing portrait a
library of literature has grown up round the figure of
Samuel Pepys. His career, his appearance, his opinions,
his habits, his illnesses, his tastes, his talents, and his
vices have been discussed with a wealth of specialised
detail which can only be equalled in the case of very
few historical celebrities. Indeed it may be said without exaggeration that there is no one in the past about
whom such a mass of intimate material is available.
But the Pepys thus pictured is the man as we know him
to-day. His career is related in the light of the Diary
and his character is read out of the pages of the Diary.
The Diary in fact has been used to illuminate the two
earlier portraits. But the Pepys as known to the world
since the mid-nineteenth century has no resemblance
whatever to the Pepys of the eighteenth century, if his
name indeed were ever pronounced then at all, and is
strikingly different from the Pepys as he was known to
his contemporaries.

In using the knowledge we now possess which was
hidden from our predecessors, not only are we apt to
give an incorrect impression of what Pepys was like
when he lived and ignore the first portrait altogether,
but in so doing we spoil the surprise and entirely unexpected sensation of the eventual revelation.

In view of Dr. J. R. Tanner's careful and authoritative volumes on Pepys's life and career, which are quite indispensable to every student of Pepys, further books on him would seem hardly to be needed. But the present volume may be prevented perhaps from being a superfluous addition to Pepysian literature and from covering yet again familiar ground if an attempt be made to approach the subject rather differently: by describing the three portraits, using for each one only the material which was available to those living in the three periods. Even so we shall have to take advantage of some of the knowledge of exterior and objective facts and some inferences which can only be derived from the Diary in order to draw our contemporary portrait.

Almost every scrap of information available with regard to Pepys has already been collected together. There is little chance of anything further of importance being discovered, although there are one or two little points, such as his relations with Sir William Petty, which appear in these pages for the first time. But it seems unlikely that any fresh light will be cast into the recesses of his life.

The question now arises as to whether the material has in all cases been properly used. This new approach to the subject, distinguishing between Pepys as he was known, roughly speaking, in the seventeenth century, the eighteenth century, and the nineteenth century, may lead through a slightly more complex analysis to a fresh estimate of the man. Men, more especially those who have public duties, instinctively cultivate an exterior for public exhibition which often may not harmonise with their private life. An analysis, therefore, which detaches the public and the private before welding them together and considers at the same time the verdict of immediately succeeding generations may have some value.

There will be no need to recapitulate all the facts about Pepys's career or to requote the multitude of details concerning every phase of his life and every facet of his character. Students of Pepys who have not these facts at their finger-ends will find many a book where they have been carefully collated and exhaustively dealt with.

In this volume an endeavour will be made to throw lights on him as a man from different angles and analyse him as diarist with more special reference to the art of diary writing.

As it is not intended to follow Pepys consecutively through his career, it will be useful for purposes of reference to give here a brief chronological table of the chief incidents in his life.

	Born February 23, 1632/33; educated at Huntingdon and St. Paul's School, London.
1650/51.	March 5, entered into residence at Magdalene College, Cambridge.
1653.	Graduated B.A.; 1660, M.A.
1655.	December 1, married Elizabeth St. Michel.
1656.	Steward to Sir Edward Montagu.
1658.	March 26, underwent successful operation for the stone.
1659/60.	January 1, Diary begins; resided at Axe Yard, Westminster; Clerk to Sir George Downing, Teller of the Exchequer.
1660.	July 13, Clerk of the Acts; moved to Navy Office between Crutched Friars and Seething Lane.
	July 23, Clerk of the Privy Seal.

1660.   September 17, sworn in as Justice of the Peace.
1661/62.   Member of Tangier Commission.
1664/65.   March 20, Treasurer of the Tangier Commission.
1667/68.   Spoke in defence of the Navy before the House of Commons.
1669.   May 31, Diary concluded.
           November 10, Death of Mrs. Pepys.
1673.   Secretary of the Admiralty; M.P. for Castle Rising.
1676.   Master of the Trinity House.
1677.   Master of the Clothworkers' Company.
1679.   M.P. for Harwich.
           May 21, Resigned Secretaryship of the Admiralty.
           May 22, Committed to the Tower (on accusation of sending information about the Navy to the French Government).
1679/80.   February 12, Discharged.
1683.   Visit to Tangier; wrote Tangier Diary.
1684.   June 10, Again appointed Secretary of the Admiralty.
           President of the Royal Society; residence, York Buildings.
1685.   M.P. for Harwich.
1686.   June, Secretary of the Admiralty.
1688/89.   End of his official career as Secretary of the Navy.
1689.   June 25, Committed to the Gatehouse; released in July.
1690.   Published Memoirs of the Royal Navy.
1701.   Retired to William Hewer's house at Clapham.
1703.   May 26, Died.
           June 5, Buried in St. Olave's Church, Hart Street.

CHAPTER I

PEPYS AS SEEN BY HIS CONTEMPORARIES

THE portrait which biography and history give us of celebrated people in all probability seldom corresponds absolutely with the contemporary estimate of the person in question. A contemporary estimate is composed of a number of fleeting and incomplete impressions, personal contacts, intimate and superficial, and the passing gossip which we all hear about one another. Most people have to stand or fall by the outside estimate made of them.

A biography is more accurate because it is more complete. But the tendency of biographers to idealise their subjects is apt to furnish posterity with a more favourable picture than that which those who lived with and knew the man or woman in the flesh would have been prepared to accept. This is more especially likely to be the case when we do not begin making our portrait till long after our subject and his acquaintances have passed away. We only began writing about Samuel Pepys over one hundred and twenty years after his death.

Considering all the books and plays and essays and articles which have been written on Pepys, round Pepys and through Pepys's eyes on the Pepysian period, it

B

becomes very difficult for us to readjust our perspective and dismiss from our imagination the sparkling, witty, naughty, attractive figure often built up out of the Diary. We have got to do something more than that. We have got to make even a greater effort than the dismissal of this image. A different man has got to be substituted if we are going to try conscientiously to reconstruct Pepys as he was seen by his contemporaries. This is well worth doing, because it is important that we should understand not only what sort of man Pepys was, but what sort of figure he presented to those who lived with him, what they thought about him, and how he fitted into the life of his times, if we are to enjoy the Diary to the full and relish the psychological surprise it presents.

Life consists not only of incidents and impressions, but of relationships. Relationships indeed may perhaps be the most significant element in human existence, more significant than acts and achievements, because they comprehend all the expressions of the individual life as shown in their own reactions. In the case of people whose biographies are written soon after their death, it is possible to rescue first-hand some account of these relationships. In the case of a man who died several generations ago this becomes impossible. However vivid it may be, the one-sided account of relationships from the point of view of the subject himself is not likely to give the full story.

The Diary gives us very little help in this first portrait of seventeenth-century Pepys. When the nineteenth-century Pepys is described, it will be shown how diaries can reveal a side of a person which is unsuspected by and quite unknown to his contemporaries.

Had Pepys possessed outwardly in his social outfit one-tenth of the perspicacity, shrewdness, wit, and charm which is shown in the Diary, he would have been spoken of and referred to by many friends and acquaintances with appreciation and even enthusiasm.

As it is, with the notable exception of John Evelyn's comments and some inevitable official references to him, he was but little more noticed than the multitude of other officials and public servants of his time. Very few people were interested in his career, which was neither sensational nor remarkable; he received, it is true, cordial commendations for his efficiency from his official superiors, but so far as the Court and high society were concerned he was a spectator, listening and observing with all his ears and eyes no doubt, but, as it happens, listeners and observers often pass quite unnoticed themselves.

As a more or less prominent permanent official Clerk of the Acts in the Navy Office (1660) and Secretary of the Admiralty (from 1673 to 1679 and again from 1684 to 1689) he was of course well known in the official world. The Civil Service has been in other instances the shelter or screen behind which in obscurity literary talent has flourished. A very notable example in recent years was Hale White, clerk in the Admiralty, who for many years was practically unknown as the author of the Mark Rutherford series of novels. But his identity was disclosed during his lifetime. This, however, is not an analogous case, because we are not dealing with an author. *The Portugal History*, by S. P., Esq., published in 1668, may be dismissed, as there is not a shred of external evidence that Pepys was the author. In any case, it is a colourless little book which could have brought fame to no one. Pepys's notes or *Memoirs of the Navy*, produced in 1690, on which comment will be made later, was purely an official, controversial pamphlet. We who have unearthed it are surprised that it is the work of the Diarist. Much more surprised would the seventeenth-century readers of the *Memoirs* have been had they seen the Diary. The little book serves as a good index of the contrast between the Pepys of the seventeenth century and the Pepys of the nineteenth century, the public servant as known to his contemporaries, the man at home as known to us now.

In 1660 Pepys was sworn a justice of the peace, for which he was "mightily pleased" though "wholly ignorant" of the duties of his position. His appointment as Treasurer of the Commission for managing the affairs of Tangier and his subsequent visit for the arrangement of the evacuation of Tangier were departmental matters known only to a small circle of officials and politicians. His very brief membership of Parliament in 1673 as M.P. for Castle Rising and in 1689 for Harwich gave him no time or opportunity to make any mark in the House of Commons even if he had had any parliamentary talent. His speeches in Parliament were the speeches of an expert full of facts and figures. The ordinary member is always irritated by the pontificial instruction of the specialist. On May 11, 1678, a member complained of Pepys's haughtiness. He "speaks rather like an Admiral than a Secretary, 'I' and 'we'".

His imprisonment for a very short time on the charge of being implicated in a Jacobite intrigue only classed him with a number of other people who were similarly

and generally far more severely treated, and the
trumped-up charge of sending information about the
Navy to the French Government was easily disposed
of. He acquired no fame from martyrdom nor indeed
did he ever seek it.

Lampoons, however ill-natured and unfair, can
give some idea of the impression which their victim
has made on at any rate a section of his contemporaries.
Like a caricature, they exaggerate existing peculiarities.
The accusation brought against Pepys that he was a
Roman Catholic in disguise was revived more than
once both in the Press and in Parliament; and at the
same time a couple of scurrilous pamphlets were
published accusing him and his clerk William Hewer
of gross corruption. That the main accusation was
groundless can be shown by several instances during
his first tenure of office as Secretary to the Admiralty,
in which he not only refused bribes, but rebuked those
who offered them, and James Houblon in a letter
referred to "those petty advantages and sneaking
perquisites your predecessors did stoop to and which
you have to your hurt rejected ". But the method of
approach in one of the lampoons, called *A Hue and Cry
after P. and H.*, shows us the sort of malicious envy
which was inspired in some quarters by Pepys's over-
ostentatious manner and habit. One of the passages
begins:

There is one thing more you might be mightily sorry
for with all speed; Your Presumption in your Coach, in
which you dayly Ride as if you had been Son and Heir to
the Great Emperor *Neptune*; or as if you had been
Infallibly to have succeeded him in his Government of the
Ocean. All which was Presumption of the highest Degree.

The pamphlets probably had but a small circulation and it would be a mistake to infer that Pepys in the days of his temporary disgrace was really an unpopular figure in London. But then he was never a popular or well-known figure either.

Unlike Greville, he was not at home in high political society, nor, like J. Wilson Croker, was he the confidant of statesmen, nor even, like Creevey, a notorious society gossip. He was a climber and had all the sensitiveness and conceit of a man rising from a humble position.

In one place Pepys admits: "But I believe indeed our family were never considerable". On the other hand, he shows pride in his descent by inscribing on one of his book-plates, "Descended from ye antient family of Pepys of Cottenham in Cambridgeshire". Scientific research into the Diarist's predecessors does not reveal anything which could have made Samuel confident of aristocratic birth. His father, John Pepys, a citizen of London, followed the trade of a tailor, and there are many remarks in the Diary showing Samuel's eagerness to rise in the social scale. He was "not a little proud" in March 1660 when he received for the first time a letter addressed "Samuel Pepys, Esq."

The strain of purely social ambition is always noticeable. His associates must have detected this strain and suspected that he was "on the make", which indeed he was. In his portraits we can observe the rather coarse geniality of one who has arrived. He was delighted at having arrived, and of course this too was noticed by his fellow-officials and friends. Climbers are never very popular, nor are hangers-on, and Pepys was both. He was bent on making a good appearance and took great pains to give the outward impression of the important person he thought himself to be. In the days of his prosperity we even find him becoming rather ostentatious in his self-importance. The innocent way in which the confessions are made excuses him to us, but this was not discernible by a contemporary outside observer. For instance, at the end of 1666 he writes:

> One thing I reckon remarkable in my own condition is that I am come to abound in good plate, so as at all entertainments to be served wholly with silver plates, having two dozen and a half;

and again concluding an entry on May 12, 1669, he says:

> Thence walked a little with Creed who tells me he hears how fine my horses and coach are and advises me to avoid being noted for it, which I was vexed to hear taken notice of, being what I feared; and Povy told me of my gold-laced sleeves in the Park yesterday, which vexed me also, so as to resolve never to appear in Court with them, but presently to have them taken off, as it is fit I should, and so called at my tailors for that purpose.

It is not unlikely that a good many people just good-humouredly laughed at him.

In his school-days at St. Paul's School and during his academic career at Magdalene College, Cambridge, nothing occurred which distinguished him from his school-fellows or fellow-undergraduates.

That he was "scandalously overseene in drink" is a fact which was only ferreted out in our nineteenth-century eagerness to discover every syllable ever uttered about him. It was in no way a remarkable fact, nor was it a special sign of dissipation; similar charges could be found against hundreds or rather thousands of university undergraduates in every generation.

That he wrote a romance in his youthful days was nothing extraordinary. *Love a Cheate* never saw the light of day, and this is not the place to quote the charming remark he made about it in his Diary.

Samuel Pepys was undoubtedly a painstaking and conscientious official. As such and chiefly as such was his reputation made in the London of his day. On this alone can we construct the image of him as it appeared to the majority of the public in Restoration times—a punctilious official with whom eminent people talked shop, a studious clerk who could be relied on to discharge his duties efficiently. Introduced into or rather promoted in official life by his kinsman, Lord Sandwich, he succeeded by his own merits in reaching a high and responsible position. Nor was he just a humdrum routine drudge. He was a reformer, an initiator, a far-sighted framer of policy. He stood out against bribery and corruption more than was usual in those days and exercised a commendable severity in administration in the face of considerable opposition. He took an advanced line on the controversy of Gentlemen *versus* Tarpaulins. He had no objection to officers because of their breeding but saw the danger of their lack of seamanship. "The general ignorance and dulness of our lieutenants of ships is a great evil." Through his efforts a reform was introduced by which lieutenants were instructed and examined. He reformed the manner of supplying chaplains to the fleet, he investigated the question of timber for the Navy, and just before his resignation he was tackling the quality of the victuals served out to seamen. "Englishmen," he writes in his Naval Minutes, "and more especially seamen, love their

bellies above anything else, and therefore it must
always be remembered in the management of the
victualling of the navy that to make any abatement
from them in the quantity or agreeableness of the
victuals is to discourage and provoke them in the
tenderest point, and will sooner render them disgusted
with the King's service than any one other hardship
that can be put upon them." Even on the technicalities
of shipbuilding his opinion was worth having.

How deeply and sincerely he had the cause of the
public service at heart is shown throughout, and more
especially in the elaborate precautions for which he
was responsible in guarding the Navy at the time of the
Popish plot. His great anxiety is shown in a passage
in a letter he wrote to Sir Richard Beach at Chatham
on November 21, 1678:

It occasioning me I doe assure you more distraction in
my busyness by day and breach of my rest by night than
all the difficulties I ever yet stood under since I had the
honour of Serveing his Ma^{tte} in the Navy.

All this, however, was only known to his immediate
associates and high officials. Charles II. often spoke
to him about "navy business", having heard of his
reputation and himself wanting, no doubt, a little coach-
ing. The Duke of Albemarle referred to Pepys as the
"right hand of the Navy". The Duke of York thanked
Lord Sandwich for having brought Pepys into the Navy
and "seemed much to rely on what I said". Sir
William Coventry, the Duke of York's secretary, was
closely concerned with naval administrations, and had
as high opinion as the others of the fitness of this
admirable official for his work.

Were we making our observations from Pepys's

point of view and not from the point of view of the others, there is many a passage from the Diary which could be quoted giving his delightfully simple satisfaction at being recognised and having masters "that do observe that I take pains". But at this point we must look from without, not from within.

Sir William Petty, as one would expect, was a man after Pepys's own heart. Pepys was a "curious" man interested in many subjects, but Petty had a far larger range, and was not content with inquiry, but wrote notes, dissertations, treatises on every conceivable subject, statistical, economic, financial, naval, scientific, religious, and social. Owing to the fact that his cousin, Sir Robert Southwell, kept every line Petty wrote to him, his papers at one time filled fifty-three chests. But only recently have they been sorted and described. Petty appears in the Diary as the inventor of the double-bottomed ship. Pepys, in spite of opposition and the King's contempt for it, was inclined to believe in the invention, although he admits the ship has "an odd appearance". But we can gather that he very much appreciates Petty's company. He refers to him as one "who in discourse is, methinks, one of the most rational men that I ever heard speak with a tongue having all his notions the most distinct and clear"; and on another occasion he says "excellent company and good discourse; but above all I do value Sir William Petty". In his Naval Minutes there are "several notes on what Petty said and thought".

Owing to the preservation of Petty's correspondence and papers,[1] this is one of the rare instances in which

[1] *The Petty Papers*, edited by the Marquis of Lansdowne, 2 vols., 1927.

we can get a little light on Pepys from the other side.

Petty wrote verses in Latin and English, but he was by no means as proud of them as he was of his other prolific productions. In a letter to Southwell he writes about some of his verses that he is "afraid to show them much lesse to print them. Lett Mr. Pepys see them if you think fitt and thank him heartily for lending a hand to rowe mee ahed in the foull weather." This shows confidence in Pepys's sense of humour and a knowledge that the Secretary of the Admiralty would not be shocked by a little frivolity. The latter part of the sentence is of course metaphorical. Petty, always determined to push his schemes, found a man in Pepys's position useful. Southwell tells him that Pepys "takes a mighty share in all you say and doe", and recommends him as a good adviser "as to sea affairs, Here is Mr. Pepys come who will be the proper object of your navall addresses in future". This was in 1684, and in the same year Petty complains to Southwell on more than one occasion that he can get no answer from Pepys. Conceivably the Secretary of the Admiralty was afraid that this strange and importunate philosopher and inventor wanted to convert the whole Navy into double-bottomed ships. But later Petty is engaged on a treatise with regard to "the multiplication of mankind", and he demands an assurance from Southwell that he has not shown it "to any fortunate fop". Southwell confesses he has shown it to Pepys. Petty replies: "I like your having shown the paper to Mr. Pepys for he is no fop though fortunate". "Fop" here is probably used in the older sense of "fool". "Fortunate" evidently refers to the high position which Pepys occupied. Thus we see the dignified official appreciated as taking an intelligent and sympathetic interest in the schemes of the enthusiastic and ingenious inventor and statistician.[1]

In the Rawlinson collection of papers there is a copy of Petty's *Dialogue between A. and B. on Liberty of Conscience, 1687*, endorsed by Pepys "Sir William Petty's paper, written at my desire, and given me by himself a little before his death". So it was by no means only the double-bottomed ships in which Pepys was interested. When Petty dies, Southwell writes to Pepys:

You will not wonder when soe great a man is fallen as our friend Sir William Petty that I should condole the losse. I had some share in his friendship, and you in his high esteeme. Soe we are both sufferers and till wee can repayre it, 'tis but reasonable that we comfort each other.[2]

This testimony to Pepys, although slight, is interesting, but we must remember that Sir William Petty in his day was himself only regarded as a crank and little attention was paid to the astonishing fertility of his imagination.

There came an occasion in March 1667/68 when for one brief day the name of Samuel Pepys was known beyond the limited circle of the Navy Office. There had been an outcry in Parliament against the principal officers of the Navy after the Dutch war. The disgrace the country had suffered by the presence of De Ruyter's fleet in the Medway led very naturally to the cry that someone should be punished. In October

---

[1] *The Petty-Southwell Correspondence*, edited by the Marquis of Lansdowne, 1928.

[2] Historical Manuscripts Commission. Fifteenth Report, Appendix, Part II.

1667 the Secretary of the Navy made his report before a parliamentary committee. But this did not end the matter, and the officers were ordered to be heard in their own defence at the bar of the House of Commons. The whole labour of the defence fell on the Secretary. For three hours, on March 5, 1667/68, Samuel Pepys spoke, after taking half a pint of mulled sack and a dram of brandy. "My speech being so long," he notes, "many had gone out to dinner and come in again half drunk." Although he had a bad case to defend, so persuasive was he that no further proceedings were taken. Praise was showered on him from the King downwards (although here again we have no authority whatever but his own). The Commons Journal merely contains a statement that the principal officers of the Navy appeared at the bar. Pepys's name is not even mentioned.

One can quite imagine, however, a permanent official with all the facts at his finger-tips being able to impress Members of Parliament whose inside knowledge of affairs must necessarily be scanty. But many a fine single speech has been made which together with its author has passed into oblivion, while the author has been far more impressed by its importance than anyone else. His name was heard of for the first time by the general or rather the London public, and probably forgotten by them a week later. The episode fired him with the ambition to enter Parliament. But although he attained his wish, no fame whatever in that sphere awaited him.

Before turning to another Pepys who was known only to a few friends, we may note at this stage how entirely different this conscientious civil servant, this

naval expert, this quiet punctilious clerk, this man of
more or less humble origin who was rising from the
ranks, this unassuming permanent official, was from
the brilliant gay Lothario which the nineteenth-century
verdict is apt to make us see in the diarist and make
us believe was the impression he gave to his contemporaries. Far from disparaging his abilities as an
official the deeper we dig the greater is our admiration
for his conspicuous administrative qualities. The
point to be emphasised is that all this was not, and
indeed could not have been, known except to a very
small number of people.

There were a few—not very many—who knew
Pepys more intimately. He did not entertain much,
because for years he could not afford to. He had his
annual dinner to celebrate his successful operation of
having been cut for the stone, and he was very sociable
—"sad for want of company and know not how to eat
alone". His private life and his official life were
separate. Few of his official associates knew what
sort of man he was at home. There is nothing unusual
in this; it is the case with public men, officials, and
business men in all periods. His private friends found
him fairly domestic, very naïve, and interested in an
immense variety of subjects of which few of them
knew anything. His childishness may have been
rather attractive. It was sufficiently pronounced for
him to be fully aware of it himself. After being given
a watch he writes:

But Lord to see how much of my old folly and childishness hangs on me still that I cannot forbear carrying my
watch in my hand in the coach all this afternoon and seeing
what o'clock it is one hundred times.

There is no justification whatever for thinking that
Pepys was a wit and a raconteur or a brilliant conver-
sationalist. He greatly enjoyed "excellent discourse",
but there is no evidence that he contributed to it.
Had he been a social success the circle of his acquaintances would have widened, and he would have gained
the same sort of reputation as a beau of a later date.
Although on the make he was naturally modest, his
manner and bearing were not those of a fine gentleman.
Being as we now know so astonishingly alert to receive
impressions, his powers of expression may have been
very limited. He may be called garrulous on paper,
but this if anything might be taken as a proof that he
was not garrulous in conversation. Many a brilliant
and witty writer has been a dull dog to meet. Many
silent people are effusive correspondents. Not one
syllable of what he said in conversation has come down
to us, and with very few exceptions no one who met
him wrote a word about him.

We have a wonderful picture of Mrs. Pepys, through
Pepys's eyes, but not a line about Samuel from his wife.
We can easily gather, however, that she was very
frequently exasperated by him, and scenes between
them were common enough. His infidelities were a
high trial for her as well as his wretched attacks of
jealousy, and there is little wonder that sometimes she
was "as mad as a devil" and had "nothing but ill
words". Yet undoubtedly she was fond of him.
They talk over in bed the old days "when she used to
make coal fires and wash my foul clothes with her own
hand for me, poor wretch! in our little room at my
Lord Sandwich's". Mrs. Pepys's point of view can be
found, although indirectly, in the entry in which he says:

So home to dinner with my wife, very pleasant and pleased with one another's company and in our general enjoyment of one another, better we think than most couples do.

A wife's impressions of her husband are by their intimacy a very valuable because unique element in arriving at a complete estimate of a man's character. But they hardly count, unless she be a diarist, a recorder, or herself a biographer, as a contribution to the general public impression which the man made on his times. Had Elizabeth Pepys left us a memoir concerning her husband it would certainly have served to accentuate the difference between the Pepys the world outside knew and Pepys at home, that is to say between the seventeenth-century and nineteenth-century portraits.

The impression his servants gained of him varied owing to his very capricious behaviour to them. But this again is of small moment in measuring his public reputation. His amours were not of a bold, dashing, and brilliant kind, such as would have made him a prominent figure with the beauties of the dissolute Restoration society. On the contrary they were surreptitious and rather sordid, and being secret neither contributed to nor detracted from his public reputation. With such ease and sparkle does he describe in his Diary the Castlemaines, the Mrs. Stewarts, the Nell Gwynns, etc., of the day that we are apt to picture him as being "in" with them all, whereas of course he was only, so to speak, looking through the keyhole.

The very detailed account of his domestic life which has a place of such prominence in the Diary has misled many readers into supposing that the Pepys thus mirrored with life-like accuracy was the Pepys that others saw. It was not. In all but the lives of very few, and certainly in all the lives of obscure and ordinary people, the curtain drawn over home life is never lifted and only partially drawn aside for a passing moment by an occasionally intimate friend.

But Samuel Pepys was President of the Royal Society. Was not this fame? In 1664 he joined the Royal Society, and in 1684 he was elected President. Not only was he a man of hobbies, but he had a genuine love of art, architecture, music, and books, without any profound knowledge of any of them. The large variety of subjects about which he had an insatiable and almost childish curiosity was not generally known. But his undoubted appreciation of art and science, coupled with his prominent official position, made him a suitable person to serve on the Council of the Society and eventually to be President. The Royal Society had only just been founded by Charles II. Although by no means addicted to intellectual pursuits, His Majesty was fond of chemistry and made experiments in his own laboratory. He was also interested in the science of navigation and the principles of shipbuilding. The range of the Society was very comprehensive, but science was in its early infancy, and the Society was still amusing itself with rather absurd experiments. When the eccentric Duchess of Newcastle visited it, "several fine experiments were shown her of colours, loadstones, microscopes and of liquors; among others of one that did while she was there turn a piece of roasted mutton into pure blood which was very rare". We must not therefore overestimate the importance of either the Society or the office of President. There

C

can be very few people who know anything at all about Pepys's predecessor, Sir Cyril Wyche.

Nevertheless Pepys's unquestionable talent as an amateur in the highest sense of the word brought him into contact with a wider circle of acquaintances than the official world. As a bibliophile and collector, and more especially as a musician, he must have made friends among kindred spirits. But his talents, although varied, were none of them conspicuous, and he was certainly not regarded in his day as an outstanding scientist, man of letters, or musician. Many a civil servant has had far more profound knowledge of science, art, and literature unknown to most of his colleagues. In the days of his retirement, first of all at York Buildings and then at Clapham with his old friend Hewer, he lived a very secluded life, making himself ill, indeed, by "my constant poreing and sitting so long in one posture without any divertings or exercise". He was busy day by day with his many occupations and collections, but so far as the outside world was concerned even his diligent work at the Navy Office had been forgotten in the turmoil of the great events which occupied the attention of the world outside.

There was, however, one man whose intercourse with him is recorded, and has been handed down to us. As this man, John Evelyn, was one of the remarkable men of the day, the relations between the two deserve special attention in a separate chapter in order to complete the seventeenth-century portrait of Pepys.

CHAPTER II

PEPYS AND EVELYN

JOHN EVELYN was a cultivated gentleman and an accomplished scholar, a man with acute artistic appreciations and rather charmingly addicted to philosophic reflections. His book *Sylva*, on forest trees, printed by order of the Royal Society, gave him considerable fame in his day. He wrote also on a large variety of subjects—on gardening, on engraving, on coins, on costume, on topography—always with profound erudition. His style was sometimes inclined to be heavy and involved, and his books did not survive long as classics, but there is ample proof to show that he was a highly respected and distinguished personality whose advice was sought and whose authority was quoted. He was thirteen years older than Pepys, and was the writer of delightful memoirs in journal form which cover sixty-four years.

We are not here concerned with the comparison of the two Diaries. Evelyn in his record referred to Pepys as for nearly forty years "my particular friend". We are able, therefore, to get a first-hand opinion of Pepys from a notable contemporary and friend, and this is of the highest importance in estimating the impression

19

which the living Pepys of the seventeenth century made
on his friends and acquaintances.

Unfortunately we find ourselves obliged to fall back
to some extent on inferences, as there is little in the
nature of a picture or even sketch. A couple of entries
from Pepys's Diary give us Evelyn to the life, whereas
all the mentions of Pepys in Evelyn's Diary collected
together tell us more of the relationship between the
two men and the subjects they discussed than of the
character, appearance, or manners of the Secretary of
the Navy. Evelyn, always a little ponderous, eschews
what he would have considered irrelevant personalities.
Nevertheless the references serve to show that outside
his official duties Pepys won for himself some reputation as a prominent amateur in artistic and intellectual
society. Moreover there are letters as well as diary
entries to refer to.

The two men noted one another in their diaries,
although neither seems to have known that the other
kept a diary: not unlike Sir Walter Scott and Tom
Moore.

Pepys notices Evelyn before Evelyn notices Pepys.
This is natural enough: not only because Pepys as a
punctilious diarist gives a more detailed account of his
day and of the people he meets, but also because
Evelyn was a prominent figure in society and Pepys
was not. But although Evelyn was of aristocratic
birth he was no snob, and was ready to make friends
with one who might be considered socially as his
inferior.

On September 10, 1665, there was a little party at
Captain Cocke's at which both were present. There
was great jubilation over the taking of the East India

prizes. Pepys's delightfully amusing account of the
entertainment gives us a sidelight on Evelyn, showing
characteristics which would never be suspected in the
staid and dignified scholar. He made them "all die
almost with laughing". Evelyn, on the other hand,
makes no mention whatever of Pepys or of the entertainment. Pepys was in the corner amused, listening
and observing, but taking no part in the contest of
wits between Evelyn and Sir John Minnes.

On November 5 of the same year Pepys visits
Evelyn at Sayes Court. This is the entry which contains the appreciative but shrewdly critical description
of Evelyn, which sums him up more completely than
a volume of biography. It ends: "In fine, a most
excellent person he is and must be allowed a little for
a little conceitedness; but he may well be so, being a
man so much above others. He read me, though with
too much gusto, some little poems of his own that were
not transcendent. . . ." The "most excellent person",
however, never wrote a line in his Diary about Pepys's
visit. In January 1665/66 Pepys notes that there was
more "excellent discourse" between them on "the
vanity and vices of the Court", and in the following
April at Sayes Court "he and I walked together in the
garden with mighty pleasure he being an ingenious man;
and the more I know him the more I love him".

Evelyn, however, had not yet been struck by Pepys's
personality sufficiently to make any reference to him
at all in his Journal. Not till June 1669, after Pepys had
closed his Diary, does the first mention of Pepys appear
in Evelyn's record. Richard Evelyn was going to be
cut for the stone. John Evelyn brings Mr. Pepys to
his brother to encourage him by showing him the stone

"as big as a tennis ball" as a proof of Pepys's successful operation.

After this there are several references to meetings and dinners, incidentally showing that Evelyn was no fair-weather friend. In 1679 he goes and dines with Pepys when he is put in the Tower, and says, "I believe he was unjustly charged"; and again in 1690, when Pepys returns from the Gatehouse where he had been confined on a charge of having sent information about the state of the English Navy to the French Court. There was no evidence against him, and he was allowed to return home on the grounds of ill-health. To his friends who bailed him from prison Pepys wrote a characteristic letter of gratitude in which there is no heroic expression of righteous indignation.

Being this day become once again a free man in every respect, I mean, but that of my obligation to you and the rest of my friends, to whom I stand indebted for my being so, I think it but a reasonable part of my duty to pay you and them my thanks for it in a body; but know not how otherwise to compass it than by begging you which I hereby do, to take your share with them and me here, tomorrow, of a piece of mutton, which is all I dare promise you besides that of my being ever
your most bounden and faithful humble servant
S. P.

Evelyn records an occasion when he expresses special interest in a book possessed by Pepys, written by Deane on the art of building ships; there is a bald record of their journey together to Portsmouth; there is a full account of the dinner, after which Pepys shows him the papers disclosing the fact that Charles II. had died a Roman Catholic; there are talks about the Navy, and there is a note of Evelyn having his portrait painted by Kneller "for Mr. Pepys, late Secretary to the Admiralty". Pepys told him he was having portraits of "the Boyles, the Gales and the Newtons of our nation". To which Evelyn modestly replies, "What, in God's name, should a planter of colewort do amongst such worthies?"

But all these entries consist purely of a bare record of fact and statement. Three times only is there anything in the nature of personal description.

In 1671 he entertains amongst others to dinner "Dr. Christopher Wren and Mr. Pepys, Clerk of the Acts", and he describes them as "two extraordinary ingenious and knowing persons". It is certainly a high compliment to Pepys that his name should be coupled with the great architect who at that time was embarking on his plans for the rebuilding of St. Paul's.

In 1700, when Evelyn was eighty and Pepys sixty-seven, he records a visit to Clapham:

I went to visit Mr. Pepys at Clapham where he has a very noble and wonderfully well-furnished house especially with Indian and Chinese curiosities, the offices and gardens well accommodated for pleasure and retirement.

Finally there is the passage in Evelyn's Diary in which he gives his obituary notice of his friend:

1703. May 26. This day died Mr. Samuel Pepys, a very worthy, industrious and curious person, none in England exceeding him in knowledge of the navy, in which he had passed through all the most considerable offices, Clerk of the Acts and Secretary of the Admiralty, all of which he performed with great integrity. When King James II. went out of England, he laid down his office, and would serve no more; but withdrawing himself from all public affairs, he lived at Clapham with his partner, Mr. Hewer, formerly his clerk, in a very noble house and sweet place, where he enjoyed the fruit of his labours in great prosperity. He was universally beloved, hospitable, generous, learned in many things, skilled in music, a very great cherisher of learned men of whom he had the conversation. His library and collection of other curiosities were of the most considerable, the models of ships especially. Besides what he published of an account of the Navy, as he found and left it, he had for divers years under his hand the History of the Navy or *Navalia* as he called it; and how far advanced, and what will follow of his, is left, I suppose, to his sister's son, Mr. Jackson, a young gentleman, whom Mr. Pepys had educated in all sorts of learning, sending him to travel abroad, from whence he returned with extraordinary accomplishments, and worthy to be heir. Mr. Pepys had been for near forty years so much my particular friend, that Mr. Jackson sent me complete mourning, desiring me to be one to hold up the pall at his magnificent obsequies; but my indisposition hindered me from doing him this last office.

This entry is all-important as being the only contemporary estimate of Pepys, and as coming from a friend who was at the same time a man of high distinction. It brings into prominence Pepys's official work, it gives him a very pleasant personal character, it makes special mention of his music, it notes his library and collections, and, although no irony is intended, it gives Pepys his true position in the learned world in describing him as "a very great cherisher of learned men of whom he had the conversation". We know "the cherishers of learned men"; they are bores, and often also diarists. Crabb Robinson, the voluminous diarist, was *par excellence* a cherisher of learned men, and very little else. They "have the conversation" of the elect, but are not among the elect themselves. Cherishers of society lights are still more frequently diarists, but seldom has their record any merit at all.

Evelyn was always generous in his estimates of friends, and seldom allowed himself to register any severe criticisms. There is something judicial in his summing up, and yet no pretence that he is writing about a remarkable man. A different note is introduced, for instance, in his eulogy of Sir William Petty, which ends, "In a word there is nothing impenetrable to him".

Letters are a useful index of a man's intercourse with his friends, and we now have Pepys's correspondence carefully edited in two volumes.[1]

In the twenty-four years from 1679 to 1703 there are hardly a score of letters from Evelyn, and fewer from Pepys to Evelyn. Evelyn's letters are most of them excellent. His pedantry is often pronounced, but there is an attractive charm in his philosophising and a genuine friendliness of tone. He certainly indulges in a certain amount of flattery more characteristic perhaps of the age than of the individual. The discoverer of Grinling Gibbons and the busy patron of art and literature was no doubt anxious to give all the encouragement he possibly could to one whose talents might be productive and whose expert knowledge might be turned to good account. The idea of the retired official collecting things of beauty and working away at his library in his comfortable "Paradisian Clapham" appealed to Evelyn, and he was evidently consoled in his depressions, which were frequent, by the company of his cheerful friend. On August 29, 1692, he writes:

Here is wood and water meadows and mountains the Dryads and Hamadryads; but there is no Mr. Pepys, no

[1] *Private Correspondence and Miscellaneous Papers of Samuel Pepys*, edited by J. R. Tanner, 1926.

Dr. Gale. Nothing of all the cheer in the parlor that I tast; all's insipid and all will be so to me 'til I see and injoy you again. . . . *O Fortunate Mr. Pepys!* who knows, possesses and injoyes all that's worth the seeking after. Let me live among your inclinations—I shall be happy.

He calls Pepys "my worthy and constant Friend"; and in 1693 he writes:

I should never forgive my selfe did I not as often remember you as I do any friend I value in the world.

In a letter dated January 20, 1702/3, in which he discussed Clarendon's *History of the Rebellion*, he ends with this warmly affectionate passage:

What I would wish for myself and all I love, as I do Mr. Pepys, should be the old man's life, as described in the distich, which you have deservedly attained:

Vita, senis, libri, domus, hortus, lectus amicus,
Vina, Nepos, ignis, mens hilaris, pietas.

In the meantime I feed on the past conversation I once had in York Buildings, and starve since my friend has forsaken it.

Several letters are devoted to encourage Pepys in his projected History of the Navy.

The noble and useful work you are meditating. . . . Will you never let us see it 'til perfect according to your scale? . . . Time flies a pace, my friend. 'Tis evening with us; do not expect perfection on this side of life. If it be the very best, as I am sure it is, nothing can be better; no man out-throws you.

He knew Pepys was well equipped by his official experience for such a bit of work; he lent him the MS. of his own history of the Dutch War. But the great book was never written. Material and notes were collected, but so formidable a task was beyond the powers and inclination of the elderly dilettante. Evelyn must have been disappointed at the little volume *Memoires of the Royal Navy* which Pepys read to him, but he was too kind to say so, and conceals his feelings in a very elaborate letter of appreciation. "So reasonable, so every way ingenuous, in so just, modest and generous a style; in a word so perfectly consummate is your excellent remonstrance and so incontestably vouched", and he amuses himself by writing out a sort of formal certificate of its merits. The friend, in fact, got the better of the learned critic and painstaking scholar. The little book had no particular merit. Pepys was too busy with his scrap-books and collections to tackle such a stiff task. Indeed he modestly admits himself that it amounts to little more than one chapter of the larger book he had in view.

If Evelyn's letters to Pepys are sometimes rather ponderous, Pepys seems to catch the same tone, and there is a noticeable strain in his endeavour to keep up to the intellectual level of his erudite friend. He does not, however, share Evelyn's depressions. "Yet I thank God too!" he says, "I have not with me one of those melancholy misgivings that you seem haunted with. The worse the World uses me the better I think I am bound to use myself."

The range of Pepys's interests was extensive, and he entered into correspondence with several distinguished men. With Isaac Newton he discusses the doctrine of chances, and Newton takes great pains in elaborating his arguments at some length. The phenomenon of second sight in the Highlands of Scotland is the subject of correspondence with Lord Reay, with the Earl of Clarendon, with his cousin and friend Dr.

Thomas Gale, High Master of St. Paul's and afterwards Dean of York, with Dr. Hickes, the deprived Dean of Worcester, and Dr. Smith, the Keeper of the Cottonian Library. To Sir Peter Pett he writes about "the par of our ancient and moderne coin both as to intrinsick value and value for use". Other subjects on which he touches always with zest are prints, book collecting, organ building, birds' nests, education, music, perspective, and micrography. His letters to his nephew, John Jackson, who was travelling abroad, which are the most numerous, are affectionate but dull. He gives much advice, urges on him "diligence in taking notes of what you meet with", and says there must be "nothing of any inferences or advisses of your own upon it, but bare matters of fact occuring to you as a traveller; and those fresh as you can at the date of your writing and so soone dispatcht as you are able when written".

In insisting on the value of a fresh impression, Pepys seems here to be remembering his own Diary; nevertheless, he never recommends his nephew to keep one. He tries to stimulate his nephew's curiosity:

In particular, it would never bee forgiven you, nor (I perswade myselfe) would you ever bee your own forgiver, should you when leaveing Italy, leave its language behind you. And as little to have omitted seeing anything of antiquity or even of moderne whose notoriety should occasion its being enquired after of you when you are come thence. I know your curiosity to be too great to suffer your falling under any such neglect; among which I cannot but reckon the Pope's Toe for one, Harry the 8th love-letters for another, and the piece of ancient painting you see imitated by our Mr. Cooke in distemper and of which Monsr Goquin gave us a copy in *taille douce*, for a third. Which last gives mee occasion for lamenting my never having given you opportunity of initiating your selfe in Drawing before your setting out hence on a journey soe full of employment for it; and for musique too. Though as to the latter I am lesse concerned, as haveing never observed your gusto much tending that way.

No detail escapes him. He calls his nephew's attention to "the ill choice of your wax on all your letters from Montpelier, as being no better than dough". He reminds Jackson, too, that as his letters must be shown to others,

Finde some way (though it be a little vulgar) to name your friends you would salute; for they generally must see your letters and it looks as if they were forgott to finde themselves never named.

All his letters to John Jackson are in the proper vein of an uncle giving instructions and advice to a dull and not particularly intelligent nephew as Jackson was. But there is ample proof that Jackson was greatly devoted to his uncle.

Pepys often writes in the vein of the persons he is addressing, almost imitates their style. Seldom if ever does he indulge in any light chaff except with his friend Sir Henry Sheeres, the military engineer, whom Pepys refers to as "a Beau". Sheeres sends him delicacies in the way of food and writes chaffingly:

The motions of great armies and expugnation of townes and provinces are the petty concerns of Princes, but to me who have greater possessions in your friendship they are lighter than vanity and the Great King of France has not more thoughtfulness about his success against so many confederate foes than I have how you may hold out against the stone and the scurvy.

Here and there a happy expression occurs in Pepys's letters, such as when he writes, "Forgive the clammyness of my memory". But on the whole it is unlikely that the correspondence would ever have been published had it not been for the Diary.

Pepys as a correspondent is indeed peculiarly unlike Pepys as a diarist, and none of his letters can have given his correspondents an inkling of the Pepys we are familiar with to-day. There is a letter, however, in which we catch a glimpse of our friend as we know him now. It shows his amused interest in something peculiar and is endorsed "a letter of compliment and banter". It is addressed to his friend Mrs. Steward in September 1695, and with this correspondent no doubt he felt released from the strain of assuming the tone of an official or of a scholar.

MADAME,
You are very good and pray continue so, by as many kind messages as you can, and notices of your health, such as the bearer brings you back my thanks for, and a thousand services. Here's a sad town, and God knows when it will be better, our losses at sea making a very melancholy exchange at both ends of it; the gentlewomen of this (to say nothing of the other) sitting with their arms across, without a yard of muslin in their shops to sell, while the ladies, they tell me walk pensively by, without a shilling, I mean a good one, in their pockets to buy. One thing there is, indeed, that comes in my way as a Governor to hear of which carries a little mirth with it, and is indeed very odd. Two wealthy citizens are late dead, and left their estates, one to a Blue Coat boy, and the other to a Blue Coat girl, in Christ's Hospital. The extraordinariness of which has led some of the magistrates to carry it on to a match which is ended in a public wedding; he in his habit of blue satin, led by two of the girls, and she in blue with an apron green, and petticoat yellow, all of sarsnet, led by two of the boys of the house through Cheapside to Guildhall Chapel, where they were married by the Dean of St. Paul's, she given by my Lord Mayor. The wedding

dinner it seems, was kept in the Hospital Hall, but the
great day will be to-morrow, St. Matthew's; when so much
I am sure of, my Lord Mayor will be there, and myself
also have had a ticket of invitation thither, and if I can
will be there too; but for the other particulars I must refer
you to my next, and do

Dear Madam, adieu

S. P.

Bow bells are just now ringing, ding, dong, but whether
for this I cannot presently tell; but it is like enough, for
I have known them ring upon much foolisher occasions,
and lately too.

His ceremonial letters are beautifully turned. This
is shown best in the correspondence with regard to
his presentation of a portrait of Dr. Wallis by Kneller
to Oxford University and also in a letter to Lord
Clarendon in which he begins:

My lord I am but this morning come from the 3rd
reading of your noble Father my Lord Chancellor Clarendon's History with the same appetite (I assure you) to a
4th as ever I had to the first.

Pepys's private correspondence gives a very good
idea of the sort of impression he made on his friends in
later life from the age of forty-six to his death, that is
to say, mostly in the years of his retirement. We gain
a high opinion of him. The expressions of affection
towards him are genuine, and it can be seen that his
"curiosity" and his disarmingly sympathetic nature
rather than his talents gave him access to the Evelyns,
Newtons, and Clarendons without any difficulty.
There is also an exchange of letters with John Dryden.
Pepys had entertained Dryden at dinner and suggested
to him that he should take the character of Chaucer's
Good Parson as a subject for a poem. The result of

this was a folio volume published in 1700 of *Fables Ancient and Modern*, a letter from Dryden offering to bring Pepys a copy of the " Character," and a reply from Pepys inviting the poet "to a cold chicken and a salad any noon after Sunday as being just stepping into the air for two days". This correspondence, which passed in July 1699, is endorsed, "Mr Dryden to S. P. upon his translating at his request Chaucer's Prologue to his Parson's Tale". The letter and the reply were inscribed in Pepys's copy of Dryden's *Fables*. We cannot, however, build up anything very much out of such incidents or letters by which Pepys receives a little reflected glory from correspondents and perhaps had some eye to collecting autographs.

No doubt the sparkle of the earlier years was dimmed by age, disillusionment, and some infirmity, and consequently a far more mellow and sedate individual is shown in the letters than in the Diary. Nevertheless, it is certain that letter writing is a very different art from diary writing, not only in the choice of subject, but in the choice of language. In writing for an immediate reader, the personality of that reader must be taken into account, ideas must be adapted and qualified, some caution may be necessary, and, in Pepys's case, the style imitated. Thus a certain restraint is imposed: this is even more the case in expressing opinions than in recording facts. Whereas the diarist, unaware of any immediate reader's eye, lets his reckless pen travel freely, governed only by his mood of the moment.

Every name that occurs in the Diary has been studied and biographical details supplied wherever possible. But many as are the mentions of statesmen, officials, courtiers, painters, and musicians, with the exception of Evelyn and to a less extent Petty, no one can be found who was at all closely associated with Pepys. He loved music, wrote one or two songs, notably "Beauty Retire", which has merit, although not quite so much as Pepys suggested by having his portrait painted with the manuscript of the song in his hand. Of the musicians he mentions none seem to have been personally acquainted with him except John Hingston, to whom he refers as "my old acquaintance". Hingston, who was a pupil of Orlando Gibbons, used to have musical meetings in his chamber, which was near St. James's Palace. But we have no contemporary criticism of Pepys as a musician, nor indeed any word of him from any of the personages the mere mention of whose names in the Diary has led to so much research.

Pepys had several books dedicated to him, but this cannot be taken as an indication of his fame. As early as 1660, "Comes in Mr. Pagan Fisher, the poet, and promises me what he had long ago done, a book in praise of the King of France with my arms and a dedication to me very handsome". Thomas Phelps, who had escaped from captivity with the Moors, published *A True Account* of his adventures and dedicated it to Pepys in 1685, and ten years later Narborough's *Voyages* was dedicated to him. Dr. Richard Cumberland's dedication of an essay to him is a splendid tribute to Pepys's constancy in friendship:

For that good affection being begun in your youth thirty years ago in Magdalene College in Cambridge, you have continued to this day, while you have gradually risen higher in the favour of our two monarchs successively and I may

D

justly reckon that nothing can break that friendship, which so great advantages of preferment on your side doth not abate.

This is a pleasant personal tribute, and several others could be found of a more or less private nature.

Before summing up and making the most of the somewhat dull colours we have for our first picture, there are one or two considerations to be taken into account concerning both men and events in the past.

Great literary figures it may be said have passed hardly recognised in their day, and posterity has been left with the most meagre and sketchy record of their lives. But their reputations have been cherished on account of their immortal creative work. Here we are dealing with a more peculiar phenomenon: a man who passed but little noticed in his day leaving no treasure from a creative mind, but supplying us with a brilliant searchlight into the innermost recesses of his own life. Of the lives of Spenser and Shakespeare very little is known. Of Pepys's personality we know more than we do of our own friends who have died recently.

We must remember, too, that, like men, events which now loom so large as historical landmarks caused nothing like the excitement which we should expect when they actually happened. Read contemporary records or diaries at the time of the loss of the Spanish Armada, read the *Gentleman's Magazine* at the time of the French Revolution, and the references to these events seem absurdly inadequate to us who with our historical perspective are able to make a very different estimate of their importance. This being the case with great men and great events, when we attempt to visualise through contemporary eyes small people, if they are visible at all, their dimensions must assume very diminutive proportions.

There is nothing surprising, therefore, in the comparative insignificance of seventeenth-century Pepys. But it is undoubtedly an interesting fact in view of subsequent events.

Taking all the foregoing facts into account, his public services, Evelyn's estimate of him, and his correspondence, being still without any clue with regard to his more intimate qualities, views, and manner of living, and having only as expression from him letters, official notes, the Admiralty Journal, and a book, all of which reached a very small number of individuals, for the most part privately, and looking through seventeenth-century eyes, what do we see?

A seventeenth-century *Who's Who*, issued, say, in the last decade of that century, would tell us of a man educated at St. Paul's and Magdalene College, Cambridge, M.A., J.P., F.R.S., M.P., author, composer, Clerk of the Exchequer, Clerk of the Acts, Clerk of the Privy Seal, Secretary of the Admiralty, Commissioner and Treasurer for the affairs of Tangier, President of the Royal Society, Governor of Christ's Hospital, Governor of St. Thomas's Hospital, Master of Trinity House, Master of the Clothworkers Company. Recreations: music, book collecting. Surely a notable personage!

But even in *Who's Who* to-day many more distinguished records may be read of men whose names are only familiar to very few, and who, admirable as their work may be, have achieved no national reputation at all. In the seventeenth century there was no *Who's Who* to remind people who Pepys was when very occasionally they heard his name mentioned. The Restoration, the Dutch War, the delinquencies of James II., the Revolution and the advent of William III. were events enough to occupy public attention without a thought being given to the minor fry who in quiet corners may have been quietly distinguishing themselves.

No, Pepys was a man of no sort of public distinction or prominence. He was merely a conscientious, a diligent official whose name was heard of in connection with the Navy as the Navy loomed large in the public eye, an expert full of departmental information and highly spoken of in the Navy, a man of no special note and perhaps occasionally seen to be rather pompously filled with the dignity of office, an associate in later days of the learned and artistic and assumed therefore himself to be learned and artistic. One of the Duke of York's minions, tarred with his brush, too cautious to be an active conspirator, one time an ambitious climber who had achieved a certain position. Again in later days a cast-off official in bad odour in retirement, said to collect curios, but only seen by a few in his seclusion. His friends tell of him as a genial companion with a sense of humour and keen power of enjoyment, one who loves a good story, and is always very ready to listen. No fine gentleman, undistinguished, and, judging by his portraits, physically unattractive; but by no means vulgar in the modern sense of the word, probably a little pretentious, fond of self-display and over-dressing; certainly no celebrity, no bearer of a name that will live, but a man occupying a niche of his own making, not on account of any genius or even talent, but because of his many aptitudes and interests and his abundant power of appreciation; not known as a collector of gossip and not condemned as a purveyor of gossip; a pleasant fellow to meet, but not impressing himself by social charm or conversation; not conspicuous in company, away there in his corner, except that a passing glance in his direction might be arrested by the unusual sparkle of his vigilant eye. A man who made no deep scratch on the surface of life in his day, but whose official integrity won for him respect in his department, whose constancy preserved for him the affection of a few friends, and whose pleasant occupations brought him to the knowledge of men of learning.

There is nothing in all this which actually clashes with or contradicts the character disclosed after a century and a quarter had passed. But the husk did not look the least like the kernel.

CHAPTER III

PEPYS IN THE EIGHTEENTH CENTURY

THE absence in the eighteenth century of any full biographical notices of men of the preceding century by no means signifies a dearth of men of note at that time. People in the eighteenth century were self-sufficient; they were interested in themselves and set but little store on the records of their predecessors, except perhaps in the more remote classical period. The art of biography of which Boswell may be said to be the English founder, and which amounts in these days to a passion, only began to flourish fully in the nineteenth century when the revival of history and archæology and the study of original documents turned men's eyes with ever-growing interest towards the past. Nevertheless there were names which were remembered and many books which were handed on. Pepys's name was not among them; in no biographical dictionary of that date is he mentioned, and nothing from his pen immediately survived him.

Samuel Pepys died at the age of seventy in 1703. He was buried in St. Olave's Church, Crutched Friars, beside his wife Elizabeth. The press notice in the London *Post Boy* for June 5 merely states:

38

Yesterday in the evening were performed the obsequies of Samuel Pepys Esq. in Crutched Friars' Church; whither his corpse was brought in a very honourable and solemn manner from Clapham.

The pall-bearers were his old friend Henry Hyde, Earl of Clarendon; Sir Anthony Deane (who like Pepys had suffered imprisonment); the honourable Mr. Hatton; the Earl of Feversham; Sir Thomas Littleton (a Treasurer of the Navy), and Mr. James Vernon (who had been Secretary of State but was for the time being under a cloud). John Evelyn, although invited, was prevented by his infirmity from being present. The Universities, the Royal Society, and the Admiralty were represented. Mourning was provided for 43 persons, and 123 rings of three different values were presented to those invited, according to their degree.

These details are quoted to show that suitable, but not excessive, pomp and ceremony accompanied the last rites to the retired official. But there the matter ended. No monument was erected to his memory. His name was quickly forgotten.

Not till 179 years later, in 1882, was Pepys accorded a special monument, which was unveiled by Mr. Russell Lowell, the American Minister, on behalf of the Earl of Northbrook, First Lord of the Admiralty, who was unavoidably absent.

What tangible evidence was left to remind the immediately succeeding generations of Pepys's existence? His portraits and his library and collections. Nothing else outside the Admiralty. Here his name and reputation lingered on, and could be revived by those who took the trouble to dig in the Admiralty archives. A commission which reported in June 1805 referred to him as "a man of extraordinary knowledge in all that related to the business of the Navy, of great talents and the most indefatigable industry". Similar eulogies could be found without difficulty of defunct officials among departmental papers.

John Jackson, with all his affection and admiration for his uncle, found nothing to present to the public in the shape of literary remains. Judging by his letters Jackson seems to have been a commonplace young man, and one wonders what he thought about the Diary. Like a dutiful nephew he undertook a revision of the catalogue of the library in 1705, so he must have come across it. Whatever qualities he may have had he certainly cannot have been endowed with his uncle's curiosity.

While written records of the later Stuart worthies may be few, their painted images abound. Lely and Kneller were kept as busy as any portrait - painters ever were. Was anyone painted as often as Pepys? Apart from Royalty it would seem doubtful. He was painted by Savil, Hales, Lely, and several times by Kneller. This does not cover the whole ground. There are several anonymous portraits among which is an excellent painting of him taken in 1687, now hanging in the official residence of the First Lord of the Admiralty. There is also a medallion by Cavalier and a bust. It would appear at first as if Pepys was determined that his name and fame should be handed down to posterity by the perpetuation of his features. There is some reason for supposing that this idea was not absent from his mind, because in his letter to Evelyn persuading him to have his portrait painted for a collection, Pepys speaks of "those few whose memories (when dead) I find myself wishing I could do aught to perpetuate". But judging by his childishly amusing remarks in the Diary when he sits to the various painters, it would seem more probable that he was just indulging one of his hobbies undertaken in the spirit of an artistic collector without much thought of posterity, or, more likely still, that he was endeavouring by this means to magnify his own importance in the eyes of his contemporaries. At any rate the scattered canvases among the plethora of portraits of that time did little or nothing to keep the memory of Pepys alive.

Again, in the exceedingly elaborate instructions he left with regard to his books and collections the idea of benefiting a grateful posterity was not so much in his mind as the collector's instinct, which is something apart. Zeal for collecting is only incidentally accompanied by any profound knowledge and is often devoid of the highest artistic sensibility. This is well illustrated by the collection in the Pepysian Library. Magdalene College possesses neither the books of a great literary light nor the collections of a great artist. But the contents of the library are eminently characteristic of Pepys as he was known in his day—the naval expert, the "ingenious" person, the "curious" man, the amusingly childish and somewhat unscrupulous collector.

So fond had he become of his collections, which occupied all his time in his retirement, and so strongly was he endowed with a sense of orderliness and neatness, that he anxiously desired that the collection should remain intact and not be broken up on his death. It had become his life's work, and it was the collection itself and not its accessibility to posterity of which he was primarily thinking. He was of course proud to act as a benefactor, and naturally turned to his old college as a suitable place for the reception of his treasures, although in the first instance they were left to his nephew John Jackson.

He began his collection in Diary days, or even before, and there are references to it in many of the entries. A few of them may be quoted.

1663. Aug. 10. Whereas before my delight was in multitude of books and spending money in that and buying alway of other things now that I am become a better husband and have left off buying now my delight is in the neatness of everything, and so cannot be pleased with anything unless it be very neat, which is a strange folly.

1664/5. Jan. 18. To my booksellers, and there did give thorough directions for the new binding of a great many of my old books to make my whole study of the same binding, within very few.

1666. July 23. Then comes Sympson, the Joyner; and he and I with great pains contriving presses to put my books up in; they now growing numerous and lying one upon another on my chairs, I lose the use to avoyde the trouble of removing them when I would open a book.

1666. Dec. 23 (Lord's day). I to my chamber and with my brother and wife did number all my books in my closet and took a list of their names which pleases me mightily and is a jobb I wanted much to have done.

But in his later days he added many more volumes, and his nephew on his travels collected for him. As late as 1701 he writes to Evelyn about "my two or three months' by-work of sorting and binding together my nephew's Roman marketings".

The library comprises a heterogeneous collection of manuscripts, curios, scraps, and books. There is Sir Francis Drake's pocket-book, James II.'s pocket-book for the time he was Lord High Admiral, a beautiful parchment manuscript roll of the Tudor Navy with coloured pictures of the ships, the first part of which was "lent" to Pepys by Mr. Thynn, "Library keeper" at St. James's, the second part given him by Charles II. It is to be feared that books and papers which were lent to Pepys were not always punctually returned. He writes to Evelyn in 1692 "in reference to that vast treasure of papers which I have had of yours so many years in my hands", and in 1700 the Secretary of the Admiralty of that day demanded the return of "several books and papers still in your custody, particularly your public Letter Books".

When he wanted something very much in the way of a book Pepys had a habit of just taking it. He would sometimes order a book for his private library and have it put down to the Admiralty account ("I think I will let the King pay for this", he explains). Mr. Gaselee [1] is probably right when he suggests that the valuable Armada book in the library, which gives lists of the ships' officers and provisions of the Spanish Armada on sheets bound together in a vellum binding, was originally preserved in the Admiralty, having come from one of the captured ships of the Armada. But it was considered by Pepys to be more suitably housed and accessible if transferred to his own private library than if it were left in the shelves of the Admiralty archives.

[1] *The Spanish Books in the Library of Samuel Pepys*, by Stephen Gaselee, 1921.

There are in the library volumes upon volumes of scrap-books in which, carefully pasted with elaborately ruled lines and inscriptions devised by Paul Lorrain, Pepys's copyist, are drawings and prints with the margins ruthlessly cut, of pastimes, views, customs, costumes, etc., etc. There are bound-up collections of tracts, of chap-books, of broadside English ballads, Spanish ballads, and Scottish poetry; there is a collection of specimens of handwriting, some of which are actually cut out from manuscript—notably a strip deliberately extracted by Pepys's scissors from the Durham gospels; and there are a number of illustrations of small writing or micrography in which Pepys was particularly interested.

Among the treasures must be mentioned a really valuable curio in the shape of a mediaeval sketch-book belonging to some English artist of the late fourteenth century, and containing rough studies of saints, birds, patterns, and grotesque figures not all by the same hand, and a most beautifully illuminated fifteenth-century manuscript of the Apocalypse.

The collection of manuscripts is very voluminous. The Sea MSS. alone consist of 114 volumes, including 11 volumes entitled *A Miscellany of Matters Historical, Political, and Naval.* In it there are copies of 1438 documents transcribed from various sources.

The books of the library, amounting to nearly 3000 volumes, repose in the cases specially designed for them. The volumes are arranged not according to subjects but according to size, the smaller ones sometimes being raised to the proper level by means of little stools of leather decorated to look like part of the binding. Larger books stand behind the smaller books and are visible above them. All this arrangement is precisely in accordance with Pepys's instructions, just as the numbering of the books, the substituted editions, the copies eliminated, etc., can all be traced to his indefatigable labours. To Pepys's many talents we can certainly add that of being a remarkably assiduous librarian, even though some of his methods may appear to be somewhat eccentric.

All the books were bound and decorated with his arms and crest, and his detailed injunctions end:

Lastly that as far as any room shall be left for further improvements or imbellishments to my books by Ruling, Elegant writing or Indexing, the same be done at the discretion and convenience of my said nephew.

There are rare volumes such as Caxtons, Wynkyn de Wordes, and Pynsons; a 1602 edition of Chaucer which he had taken to "the clasp maker's to have it clasped and bossed"; a number of books the purchase of which can be traced to Diary days; and many more which were collected rather indiscriminately in the days of his retirement. His nephew brought back many treasures for him from abroad, such as copies of Henry VIII.'s letters to Anne Boleyn, and many prints. But not all his treasures were put in the library. To John Jackson, his nephew, personally he bequeathed "all my pictures, beds, hangings, linen and all my other household goods and furniture". Through Jackson the valuables have descended to the Pepys Cockerell family, and are a testimony to the descendants of his family that Samuel lived in great style and had valuable possessions. In addition to two portraits of himself there are portraits of John de Witt by Jan de Baen and of James II. by Kneller, Verrio's original drawing for a picture of Christ's Hospital, ivory chessmen said to have been given him by James II., "a fair state dish of silver and cup with my arms ready cut upon them worth, I believe, about £18 which is a very noble present" from Sir William Coventry, and his wife's pearl necklace, the buying of which he records:

In the evening my wife being a little impatient I went along with her to buy her a necklace of pearl which will cost £4 : 10. which I am willing to comply with her for her encouragement.

Many who possess pearls and plate and pictures are perhaps rather liable for that very reason to over-estimate their own importance. So far as the library is concerned, it would be a mistake to suppose that Pepys only valued the bindings and titles and never examined the inside of his books. He read and expressed opinions on what he read, as we shall see when we reach the Diary. His library is, however, certainly the work of a collector, not a literary man, a very childish and rather capricious collector. His own little volume, to give it its full title, *Memoires relating to the State of the Royal Navy of England for ten years Determin'd December 1688*, is of course on the shelves. A conscientious student might also have discovered his Naval Minutes. These were notes and memoranda jotted down at different times by Pepys himself, and copied into the volume by clerks, with corrections in Pepys's own hand, between 1680 and 1696. They include statements, reports of fact and opinion, queries and suggestions for further consideration. They constitute the notes for the great history of the Navy which he projected but never wrote.

These Naval Minutes, had they been collected and

examined in the eighteenth century, would certainly have given people more knowledge of the Secretary of the Admiralty than they could gain from the purely official records. While of course no faint vision of the diarist is discernible, there is no doubt that in hasty jottings of opinions, reflections, and items of information, Pepys was freer and more natural than when he settled down to write a book. In scribbling down or dictating formless phrases and passing thoughts on loose pages, he approaches rather nearer to the diarist than when, as in his little volume, he strains to observe the conventions and to conform to the recognised style of an authority.

The notes cover an immense unsystematised field of observations both historical and contemporary; they show the range which it was his ambition to cover. The critical note prevails, and the controversial note is not absent. Some are desultory and even childish; others are shrewd and show the germs of larger and often wise ideas. He repeatedly makes notes deploring the want of respect and attention which the Navy received and the small recognition of seamen's services. Such an observation as the following appears frequently in different forms:

Gather instances of the little respect paid in England to the services of its sea officers; nothing done in honour of their memory. Very little provision made for their families, and the little that there is, very ill paid.

The relations of Parliament to the Navy are commented on often. He considered Parliament an unsuitable body to supervise naval administration. So highly does he rate sea experience that he makes the following suggestion:

Were it not to be wished that the seamen's trade might be made so honourable and profitable as that not only the younger brothers of England might be encouraged to seek their fortunes that way, as they hitherto have generally done (at home and abroad by trailing a pike etc. in land-service for the sake of the latter) but that even the elder might esteem it, for the dignity of it, no diminution to their qualities or estates (whatever they may be) to do the same for a voyage, or two, but on the contrary have it solemnly made a principal (if not a necessary) step towards their advancement to the greatest offices of State and Court, and to carry with it the public credit of being one of the first qualifications in a nobleman or gentleman for public trust, in Parliament or elsewhere, to have taken this degree in that great article of our English Government (hitherto so little understood and so dearly paid for) which relates to the sea, and the truth as well as importance of its interest therein.

The status of seamen abroad, both in France and Holland, is commented on favourably:

Note also with respect to the Dutch that less pay and certain is better to a seaman and his family than long and uncertain though bigger.

A few random quotations from his briefer notes will give some idea of the immense range he intended to cover:

Look over the first volume of D'Aveti's six volumes of the World; things being in it very useful.

Look into the story of Dunwich on the coast of Suffolk swallowed up by the Sea and said to have been heretofore a great place.

Q. where to read and compare the proprieties of the several tutelar saints of countries.

Consider the Act for the preservation of timber in the Forest of Deane.

The shift the Greenlanders make with their boats seems

as wonderful as anything in our shipping. Examine the true history of those people.

Has any physician in any age offered a remedy against sea-sickness?

That Pepys intended to begin from the very beginning is indicated by a dissertation he makes on Noah's ark. He wants to find out more about its construction, why it took so long to build, how carpenters and caulkers were found to do the work, why there was "all that ado for the preserving of one little family", and, lastly, how it was that anyone agreed "to see this means of safety enjoyed by so few persons and oxen and asses, suffering the universality of mankind to perish without contention for a share in it". On which questions we fear his curiosity could never have been satisfied.

The controversial note was going to be introduced, as indeed it was in the *Memoires*. We read, for instance:

The folly and malice of him that would infer my being of the French faction from my being able to give the Parliament an account of their fleet.

While some entertainment and respect for the official can be derived from the perusal of these Minutes, they never suggest the scaffolding for a great book. Whether he was baffled by the magnitude of his task and kept on recalling Evelyn's words to him, "It is not imaginable to such as have not tried what labour an historian (that would be exact) is condemned to. He must read all good and bad and remove a world of rubbish before he can lay the foundations"; or whether the far less exacting and to him more attractive occupation of collecting occupied his time to the exclusion of all other work, at any rate the book was never written,

E

and the notes and queries in the form in which they were found have only relative interest in connection with Pepys the Diarist, and we may safely say were never looked at in the eighteenth century.

In the midst of the valuable lumber of books and scrap-books, prints and curios, six manuscript volumes written in shorthand lay undisturbed with the dust gathering on them for over a hundred years. Considering that Evelyn's full Journal in longhand, easily read and accessible, remained forgotten in his family shelves from his death in 1706 until 1818, it is not surprising that eighteenth-century students should never have taken the trouble or had the curiosity to find out what was hidden in these ciphered pages.

On Jackson's death in 1724, the library was placed in a large room in the front of the Pepysian buildings, where it remained till 1849. For five years subsequently it was removed to the Master's Lodge, and since 1854 it has been beautifully arranged and carefully preserved in a fire-proof room in the Pepysian buildings. Even in the mid-nineteenth century visits to the library were made difficult by a regulation that every visitor had to be accompanied by a Fellow of the College. In the eighteenth century there is nothing to show that visitors were frequent. Very seldom does it appear to have been consulted. On one occasion, however, not only was the library visited, but the Diary was incidentally "found" and drawn attention to. In 1728, one Peter Leicester, who was interested in shorthand, went there to examine the books on the systems of shorthand. He wrote as follows to his friend John Byrom, a shorthand expert, who had himself invented a system.

I spent the last week at Cambridge. Whilst I was there I went to see a curious collection of books bequeathed to Magdalen College by the late Mr. Pepys. In the catalogue I met with a book entitled "Shorthand Collection" and would gladly have seen it but the gentleman who showed us the library being a stranger and unacquainted with the method of the catalogue, could not find it. Mr. Hadderton tells it is a collection of shorthand books containing above a hundred and fifty different methods. In searching for this book we found five large volumes, quarto, being a journal of Mr. Pepys; I did not know the method but they were writ very plain, and the proper names in common character. If you think it worth while to make Cambridge on your way to London you will meet with these and I doubt not several other shorthand curiosities in the Magdalen Library. I had not time, and was loth to be troublesome to the library keeper otherwise I would have deciphered some of the journal.

John Byrom was not only a shorthand expert, but the writer of a journal which he kept in shorthand. Had he fallen in with Leicester's suggestion he would have undoubtedly had strong sympathy with Pepys's method of journalising. Byrom in 1726 gives an excellent explanation of his own motive in keeping a journal:

I find that though what I set down in this kind of journal is nonsense for the most part yet that these nonsenses help to recollect times and persons and things upon occasion and serve at least to some purpose as to writing shorthand; therefore I must not, I think, discontinue it any longer, but only if I have a mind omit some trifling articles; though when I consider that it is the most trifling things sometimes that help us to recover more material things I do not know that I should omit trifles; they may be of use to me though to others they would appear ridiculous; but as nobody is to see them but myself, I will let myself take any notes, never so trifling, for my own use.

What if Byrom had followed Leicester's advice, if he had discovered the key to the shorthand, if he had

settled down to work and, say about 1730, produced a
complete transcript of the Diary! It is an interesting
speculation to imagine what sort of reception such a
book would have had in the days of George II. The
publication would have been too late to have amused
or interested any who actually knew Pepys personally,
and too early for it to have had any aroma of antiquity.
It might have had a certain *succès de scandale* in showing
up the Court of the later Stuarts, but most certainly it
would never have received anything like the same
appreciation of its peculiar merits which has attended
the Diary in the later nineteenth and more still in
the twentieth century. The very language of it would
have had none of the charm it has for us. Moreover,
curiously enough, each generation is inclined to be very
contemptuous of its immediate predecessor.

But Leicester passed on, Byrom ignored the suggestion, and the volumes were returned to their dusty
corner.

As to the various collections in the library, age has
given them interest and value. Two hundred years
ago they naturally did not receive much attention.
Tracts, leaflets, costume pictures, and views of late
nineteenth-century London and a collection of editions
a hundred years old would not attract students or
historians to-day. Far less so in the eighteenth century
would a number of such recent antiquities excite
curiosity, although some of the Naval MSS. seemed
to have been consulted by Admiralty officials. So
after 1724, when the library was housed at Magdalene
College it cannot have made any stir. We, the vast
army of Pepysian admirers, see it as the two-hundred-
and-fifty-year-old collection of the most famous British

Diarist. They, the few dozen who knew of its existence, saw it as the fifty-year-old collection of a Government official whose name conveyed little or nothing to them. We, Diary in hand, can trace and check the purchases, the arrangements, the peculiarities, the preferences, the taste of the donor. The College Fellows of the day knew something about the injunctions in the will, but that was all; and no one else knew anything about it nor cared.

The sensational discovery of a detailed and authentic record endows every stock and stone the writer of that record saw or touched with a new value and special significance. But we must not expect those who have not made the discovery to be moved as we are. There was the library's name. But generations of under-graduates and dons pronounced it without knowing more about Pepys than their fellows at Oxford knew, or as a matter of fact know now, about Bodley or Ash-mole. Yet Elias Ashmole, the donor of the Ashmolean Museum, was also a benefactor, an antiquary, and a diarist, who deserves better recognition if only for the fact that he tells us in his diary, "I hung three spiders about my neck and they drove my ague away".

Nevertheless, the name of an institution does nothing to perpetuate a man's memory. Men live by their works and by their deeds, in their books, in their accom-plishments, in their compositions, and in the great legacies of the creative arts. They do not live on in gifts and endowments in paintings, monuments and institu-tions; their name may continue, but if nothing else survives, their fame perishes.

Our eighteenth-century portrait becomes as the de-cades pass a more and more faded and obscured outline of a forgotten figure, until in the first quarter of the nineteenth century, before the dazzling dawn of Pepys's renascent fame, except for the library's name and the almost obscured inscriptions on the labels of some of his painted portraits, he had passed completely into oblivion.

Pepys in fact at first shared the common fate of all of us who do not lodge on the slippery pinnacle of fame. Comfortably wrapt in oblivion so far as men's minds are concerned, the tiny strand of our influence rests undetected and our name remains undiscovered in the registers of the dead. For over a century the Admiralty official had this undisturbed rest; and then suddenly he was lifted up with acclamation on to the higher peaks of the pinnacle. Tutankhamen, of whom not one man in a million had ever heard, became suddenly, after over three thousand years, a name on all men's lips for a time, not because of anything he had done, but on account of the rich and gorgeous treasures found in his death-chamber. Pepys, after a hundred and fifty years, has been placed on a more permanent national pedestal because of the still richer treasure of his own written record. For its discovery no spade was needed. The record lay there waiting until human curiosity was sufficiently sharpened to reveal its secrets.

CHAPTER IV

THE RESURRECTION OF PEPYS

THE third picture of Pepys began to be constructed in the second quarter of the nineteenth century.

In 1818 appeared the first print of Evelyn's Diary. The mention of Pepys in it attracted the attention of George Grenville, Master of Magdalene, who, we may suppose, therefore knew little or nothing till then of the donor of the library. He took the volumes of the Diary from their dusty resting-place and showed them to his kinsman Lord Grenville, the Secretary of State for Foreign Affairs. Lord Grenville, who knew something about ciphers, did a little bit of the deciphering and encouraged the Master. In 1819 the volumes, with a few hints from the Secretary of State, were handed to an undergraduate, John Smith, who immediately set to work. Smith, who eventually became rector of Baldock in Hertfordshire, wrote in 1858 an account of his task:

In the Spring of 1819 I engaged with the late Master of Magdalene College, Cambridge (I then being an undergraduate of St. John's) to decipher the whole of the Diary from the six closely written volumes of the original shorthand M.S. little thinking how difficult, how laborious, and how unprofitable a task I had undertaken. The distinguished stenographer the late William Brodie Gurney to whom I showed the M.S. at the outset, positively assured me that neither I nor any other man would ever be able to decipher it; and two eminent professors of the art confirmed his opinion. I persevered nevertheless; and in April 1822 I completed the deciphering of the whole Diary having worked for nearly three years at it usually twelve and fourteen hours a day with frequent wakeful nights. The M.S. extended to 3.012 pages of shorthand which furnished 9.325 pages in longhand and embraced 314 different short-hand characters, comprising 391 words and letters, which all had to be kept continually in mind, whilst the head, the eye and the hand of the decipherer were all engaged on the M.S. Much of it was in minute characters, greatly faded, and inscribed on almost transparent paper, very trying and injurious indeed to the visual organs.

There is a note of martyrdom in this letter, a curious absence of any appreciation of the result of his work, and no enthusiasm whatever with regard to the contents of the Diary. "Unprofitable" does not of course refer to any lack of success in the public reception of the printed Diary, but to the inadequate remuneration he thought he had received for his work.

John Smith worked at one time as a reporter on the *Cambridge Chronicle*, and for a few years was Deputy Esquire Bedell. His colleague in that post, Henry Gunning, does not seem to have formed a favourable opinion of him. In his reminiscences (1855) he refers to Smith's vulgarity, which he says was com-bined with "a flippant assurance peculiarly his own". He also accuses him of getting "a puff direct" inserted in the newspapers in which the following passage occurred:

But to whom are we indebted for deciphering this manuscript? We understand the credit of it is entirely due to the Rev. W. J. Smith, Curate of ―― in Norfolk. And is this man still a Curate? It will be a disgrace to the Bench of Bishops if he long remains so.

While John Smith was labouring away almost day and night and straining his "visual organs", on the shelf close at hand was Pepys's manuscript in shorthand with a transcript in longhand of the account taken down from the King's own lips of the story of his escape after the battle of Worcester. Here was a convenient key to the shorthand used in the Diary. Nor was this all. Thomas Skelton's *Tachygraphy*, giving a full explanation of this particular system of shorthand, was also on the shelves of the library. But so little were the books known or looked at that neither the Master nor the Fellows of the College knew of the existence of this key, which would have saved Smith weeks if not months of labour.

In 1825 Lord Braybrooke, who was Visitor of Magdalene, issued the first edition in two volumes and a second edition three years later. In the version given the Diary was much abridged and expurgated, and on this account sharply criticised. But although further editions appeared in 1848 and 1854 no substantial additions were made. In 1875 another clergyman, the Rev. Mynors Bright, undertook to decipher the whole manuscript afresh, and enlarged editions appeared. But still one-fifth of the Diary remained unprinted. Finally, in 1899, the great eight-volume edition, edited by H. B. Wheatley, was completed. In this the whole Diary was given " with the exception of a few passages which cannot possibly be printed". The Tangier Journal was also deciphered and included in 1841 by J. Smith in *The Life, Journals, and*

Correspondence of Samuel Pepys, but it has never since been reprinted.

1825 is the date, therefore, when men began asking, Who is this Samuel Pepys? and except perhaps for the Fellows of Magdalene College and a few Admiralty officials there certainly was no one who could answer that question. The door of oblivion, for which in the case of millions there is no key, was unexpectedly opened, and there emerged from the darkness not a grubby clerk nor an ailing and half-blind old antiquary, but a gay and smiling figure decked out, it must be admitted, in rather "fancy" dress, but immediately captivating, although his appearance at first was somewhat dim. Serious attention was at once accorded to him. People, so to speak, turned round and took notice, asked who he was, laughed and insisted on hearing more from him. No less a person than Sir Walter Scott reviewed the volumes in the *Quarterly* of January 1826.

It is interesting to note that Scott himself only the year before, at the age of fifty-four, had begun to keep a diary of which he was "enamoured". A more sympathetic reviewer could not have been found, because he appreciates the particular value of diary writing. This faculty, judging by the way many diaries are edited and reviewed, is by no means the general rule. After quoting the little rhyme which he has put for the motto on the first page of his own diary—

> As I walked by myself
> I talked to myself,
>   and thus myself said to me,

he proceeds:

It is no doubt certain that in this species of self intercourse we put many tricks upon our actual and our moral
self, and often endeavour to dress deeds, enacted by the
former on very egotistical principles, in such a garb as may
in some degree place them favourably before the other's
contemplation.   Still there must be more fair dealing
betwixt ourself and our conscience than ourself and anyone
else;—*here* there is much which can neither be denied or
extenuated; *Magna est veritas et prevalebit*.   Indeed such
seems the force of the principle of sincerity in this sort of
self communing as renders it wonderful how much such
records contain of what is actually discreditable to the
writers.

The varied qualities of the Diary are fully discussed,
and appreciative comments made on many of the well-
known passages.   Scott notices and is amused at the
difference between Pepys in his letters and Pepys in
his Diary, that is to say, between Pepys as he appeared
to others and as he reveals himself.   "The reader may
be amused", he says, "with comparing the style of
Pepys and his sentiments as brushed and dressed, and
sent out to meet company, with his more genuine and
far more natural effusions of a night gown and slipper
description."   Had the reviewer seen the whole Diary
he would have found this contrast still more striking.

Scott indeed saw that the two volumes did not
contain the whole story.   He deplores the use of "the
pruning knife", and rightly says "the editor will
generally speaking best attain his purpose by giving a
literal transcript of the papers in his hands; whatever
falls short of this diminishes, to a certain degree, our
confidence in the genuine character of his materials".
It was some years before the full transcript appeared.
The demand for it arose out of the recognised excellence of the abbreviated material originally given.

Lord Braybrooke in these first two volumes which were
the first heralds of Pepys's fame gave a sketch of the
author's life. This was much needed, as the general
public knew nothing whatever about him. But the
noble editor and the eminent reviewer gave a good
send-off to Pepys in the third period of his renewed
existence which was to be the overshadowing period of
his fame. From that day to this, that is to say, for over
a hundred years, the interest in Samuel Pepys has continued to increase, and the fascination of his confidences
has been felt by each succeeding generation.

Since 1825 not only have successive and increasing
full editions of the Diary been issued, but Pepys's
whole correspondence and his Naval Minutes have
been published, his library and collections have been
catalogued and classified, his illnesses analysed by
prominent physicians, a book written on his music,
the sites of his houses searched for, his friends and
acquaintances described, his own relations and his
relations by marriage unearthed, his servants' genea-
logies extracted from registers, estimates made even
of his stature calculated in relation to a giantess
he once went to see, his accounts preserved in the
strong-room of a bank, biographical notes drawn up
of everyone he mentions, every line of his character
dissected, a monument erected to him, and the history
of his times rewritten. His most casual scribbles and
unimportant notes have received an amount of attention out of all proportion to their intrinsic merits; no
line is missed, no syllable dropped. It reminds one
of the comedian who when he asked for the salt at
dinner sent the whole company into hysterics of
laughter. A hall-marked reputation seems to absolve

people from exercising their ordinary powers of discrimination.   In our twentieth-century love of documentary evidence we are likely to carry this dissection
and analysis a stage farther.   In the meanwhile
Pepysian literature, as the incomplete bibliography
attached to this volume will show, is assuming very
extensive proportions.

So it is that, with the brilliant lantern of the Diary,
an endeavour is made to reconstruct the life, habits,
and pursuits of the man with an attempt at almost
scientific accuracy by means of an abundance of
material which hardly exists in the case of any other
historical figure.   The Diary which was the origin of
all this study and research has been taken as the
foundation and the starting - point.   The colourlessness and lack of special interest in most of the
material outside the Diary has been disregarded
because it could be illuminated and given significance through the Diary.   And so the Diarist has
emerged triumphant.

The painstaking departmental official and the
collector of curios in retirement of the seventeenth
century and "someone called Pepys" who left a library
to Magdalene College and whose portraits were noticed
by a very few here and there, of the eighteenth century,
have been transformed into a fascinating, brilliant,
humorous, shrewd, rather wicked observer, a historian
indeed who is now established as one of the most
popular figures in all English history.   As he is, of
course, the central figure in his own Diary he is apt
incorrectly to become the central figure of the world
he has revealed to us in it.

The story is a surprising one; but no one would

have been more surprised at the fate that awaited him a hundred and fifty years after his death than Pepys himself. The method which has been adopted was very natural. The sensation caused by the publication of the Diary made this particular treatment of his life and career more or less inevitable. But the use of the brilliant light of the lantern to illumine the periods of darkness which preceded its lighting, by depriving us of the sequence of shadow and light, takes away something of the brilliance of the light and prevents us from appreciating to the full the surprise of such brilliance following such darkness. In fact we have spoilt the story in our excitement over the *dénouement*. We have asked people to read a mystery tale giving them the clue before they start. We are so delighted at the discovery of the last volume that we have rewritten the whole book, telling readers of the end in the preface and even relieving the dullness of the early chapters by constant references to what is coming.

Moreover, there is another consideration and an important one which shows that this treatment of the Pepysian episode is misleading. While the Diary is of course Pepys, it is not the Pepys which anyone saw. Only a close student of diaries can fully understand what this signifies. Indeed it requires a close student of diaries to estimate fully the superlative value from the psychological and human point of view of Pepys's record.

Before comparing the Diary with other diaries, which is the proper way of arriving at a right conclusion with regard to its value, a word may be said on the habit some diarists have of revealing secretly in the pages of

their private record qualities and characteristics unknown to and undiscovered by their contemporaries.

Perhaps the most notable instance of unexpected
self-revelation is afforded by the diary of William
Windham, the statesman. He was known as a brilliant
orator, a popular good-looking and successful man,
and a notable scholar. In his diary, which ignores his
parliamentary triumphs and passes over in silence
most of his famous friends, he reveals himself as an
introspective, morbid, and depressed self-analyst
addicted to fits of self-depreciation and dejection and
to curious tricks of which one was making elaborate
mental mathematical calculations. So different is the
individual thus revealed from the person as he was
popularly known that the publication of the diary has
been condemned as having dealt a mortal blow to
his reputation. It would seem, however, far more
interesting to know the whole man from the inside as
well as from the outside than to leave him on a pedestal
constructed out of ignorance of his whole nature.

Cardinal Manning's diary also exposed failings and
weaknesses in a public character who was supposed to
be devoid of them. Samuel Wilberforce, whose public
manner was that of a worldly courtier, statesman, and
popular preacher, confided to his diary gnawing sorrows
which were ever present in his mind though unsuspected by his friends ("They think me hurried with
business. They do not know that my heart is in
Lavington Church"). In the case of diaries of obscure
and unknown people we have no means of telling what
their friends thought of them; but, judging by the
intimate nature of the revelation they make in their
diaries, the self revealed would in many cases have

undoubtedly surprised the friends who knew the writer. There is no need to talk of a diary revealing the real man. The outward impression is just as much the real man. We know a side of ourselves which other people do not know, but our perspective is restricted and one-sided, and we do not see all of ourselves. Pepys the punctilious official is just as much Pepys as Pepys the Diarist. By means of his pages of self-revelation he has shown us a side which would other-wise have been hidden for ever. It so happens that the side he revealed, or, more strictly speaking, the method he adopted for revealing that side, is what has given him fame, and by means of it his official diligence has been brought to light.

Judging by his portraits, so exceptionally numerous and executed by the leading painters of the day, by his library and collections about which there are so many elaborate injunctions and regulations, by his Diary the existence of which he could not have ignored and which was subsequently bound, having been saved by him when arranging and burning old papers, "that I may have nothing by me but what is worth keeping and fit to be seen if I should miscarry" (although his entrusting the precious pages to a binder is a matter of some surprise), was Pepys after all intentionally and with careful premeditation building up a claim to posthumous fame? Did he feel sure that in the fullness of time what he had left would suffice to rank him among the world's celebrities?

It is just worth while to ask this question in order to dismiss it. The man who, failing to make the mark he would like in his lifetime, endeavours to claim the approbation and applause of posterity does not behave as Pepys behaved. In Pepys there is no symptom of calculation. Spontaneity is the essence of the man. Apart from the paintings and the library (both of which can easily be accounted for, as has been already shown), the Diary has no line in it which could justify the supposition that he knew what he was writing would bring him eventual fame. On the contrary, if he ever reflected on the matter at all, he must have had some doubt whether the Diary might not injure the reputation he was anxious to gain as a "very worthy " person, a distinguished official, a man of learning, and indeed a respectable member of society.

Pepys made no attempt at self-portraiture nor at self-justification. He was not like Sir John Reresby (1634–1689), who deliberately wrote himself up for future generations; nor like Bubb Dodington (1749–1761), who wanted to present his sordid intrigues to posterity in a favourable light; nor like Wilfrid Blunt (1888–1913), who spoiled an otherwise excellent diary by a controversial note of the self-justification which led him to publish what he had written in his own lifetime.

Again some diarists by introspection think they are delineating their characters with psychological accuracy for the benefit of those who come after. Pepys was not one of these. The self-regardant man is seldom perfectly honest. He dwells on the faults which are not very discreditable and passes over those which would show him up in a really unfavourable light. As Gladstone put it, "I do not enter on interior matters. It is so easy to write, but to write honestly nearly impossible". Of Pepys's success in this connection something will be said later. Gladstone's diary was not a good one. Few celebrated people have kept diaries of any interest; most of their journals are disappointing, whereas many quite obscure people have earned post-humous fame on account of their private journals. What a humble figure was Samuel Pepys in his time compared with Lord Sandwich, the Duke of Albe-marle, Lord Clarendon, Sir William Coventry, Lord Brounker, Stillingfleet, Thurloe, etc.; but to-day for one person who could recount anything of any one of these there are a thousand who know Pepys intimately.

Between the Pepys of the seventeenth century and Pepys of the Diary there are no actual contradictions. The amplification of his character is a revelation, but there is no impossible discord. Evelyn would have been surprised and shocked had he read the Diary, and had he undertaken to write a life of Pepys, and been handed the volumes, deciphered, as part of his material, his blue pencil would have been ruthless and some pages might have been committed to the flames. With the vision of the staid expert official and learned bibliophile in his mind, in both of which capacities he good-naturedly over-estimated his excellent friend, imagine Evelyn's feelings if he had discovered that on February 8, 1668 (the day on which Pepys had written him a grave and eloquent reflection on the Dutch War and a weighty condemnation of the proceedings in the House of Lords), his friend had written in his Diary:

To the Strand to my booksellers and there bought an idle, rogueish French book, *L'escholle des Filles* which I have bought in plain binding, avoiding the buying of it better bound, because I resolve as soon as I have read it, to burn it, that it may not stand in the list of books, nor among them, to disgrace them if it should be found.

Or again if he had read such an entry as this:

One thing of familiarity I observed in my Lady Castel-
maine; she called to one of her women for a little patch
off of her face and put it into her mouth and wetted it and
so clapped it upon her own by the side of her mouth, I
suppose she feeling a pimple rising there.

The frivolity of noticing such an incident would have
pained the author of *Sylva*, but the indecency of recording it would have grieved him still more. But this is
nothing to other parts of the Diary, which would have
completely upset him.

Had Charles II., however, been shown it he would
have been delighted, and would have found more subjects than the Navy on which to discourse with the
Clerk of the Acts. But only Sir William Coventry was
told in an unguarded moment of its existence; and he
no doubt thought his punctilious subordinate was
merely keeping a dry record of official business.

Pepys did no more than many do. In course of time
he cultivated a manner and bearing which was socially
and officially useful and suitable. He thought the
impression he was making was dignified and well
adapted to his position. He says himself that "high
carriage" will do him good, and he must appear "in
good clothes and garb". He studied the impression
he was making on others perhaps more than the average
man, because as a climber, a very creditable climber,
he was not quite at his ease for a while, and therefore
the correct manner, exterior, and appearance he cultivated was somewhat self-conscious and artificial. This
is shown in the pomposity of his portraits and explains
the incomplete and in some ways incorrect estimate of
him probably formed by his contemporaries.

But underneath and behind this exterior he was thinking and feeling as the natural man. We have now learned what our predecessors could not even guess at.

Although practically all there is to be known about Pepys is available, nevertheless the first quarter of the twentieth century has shown a steady increase in Pepysian literature. There is in short no figure in history or literature on whom a biographer or essayist would more certainly know that his volume would not be the last word.

Whether there is a lack of proportion in all this, whether our friend is receiving a great deal more attention than he merits, need not be discussed. The very strange and surprising facts are before us, and as the Diary is the cause of it all, it requires special attention and examination.

CHAPTER V

THE DIARY

THE motive which induces a person to keep a diary varies almost with each individual. Some are taught in early youth, some find an example they wish to imitate, some are compelled in their youth to write for religious disciplinary purposes, some out of business-like method keep accounts, memoranda, and engagements which gradually expand into a diary. With others again "the itch to record" starts them, and the habit once acquired is likely to remain.

Literary men in their initial steps are sometimes influenced by the writings of others from whom they receive inspiration or whose style they attempt to imitate. This is rarely if ever the case with diarists.

Pepys could have read no model diary which encouraged him to begin the practice. Edward VI.'s official recital of public events, Dr. Dee's occult notes, Lady Hoby's domestic entries, and Lady Anne Clifford's "the memorial of the life of me" could not have come under his notice, and the political diaries of Sir Simonds d'Ewes and the attractive domestic record of Sir Henry Slingsby were not available for the ordinary reader. Diary writing was in fact in its infancy although no doubt it was privately practised in many cases in which the results have been lost or destroyed. Few diaries of an earlier date than Pepys's have survived, but the habit of keeping a diary was probably more common than we imagine and was enjoined on young and old alike primarily for purposes of religious self-correction. It is interesting to note that although Pepys left off, or rather was obliged to leave off, keeping a diary, his nine years' effort converted him to the merit of diary keeping, and it is therefore a matter of some surprise that when he found that his eyesight was not permanently damaged he did not resume the practice except for the brief Tangier Diary. But other instances could be quoted of diaries which have terminated abruptly for no apparent reason. The resumption of diary writing after a long interval seems to be too great an effort, a greater effort indeed than the initial start.

In his Naval Minutes there are two notes which are interesting in connection with the value he placed on keeping a diary. He writes:

My known care in obliging captains to keep journals.

In several of his official letters he requires commanders to send up their journals. Of course this may not amount to anything more than keeping a log-book, but the very next note in the Minutes says:

And my known encouraging the Blue coat boys to do the like.

An advocacy of the practice combined with complete reticence with regard to his own record is just what would be expected from a diarist such as Pepys.

In January 1659/60, when the Diary as we have it begins, Pepys was twenty-six years old. The first

question which occurs to a careful analyst of diaries is :
Was this the first volume or the first year of writing?

The preliminary note before the first entry on
January 1 is written on a left-hand page after three
blank pages. This note might at first lead one to
suppose that he wrote a sort of Preface to the Diary.
But at the beginning of the next year, 1660/61, there is a
similar note in just the same form stating his residence,
a few remarks about the state of public affairs, and a
word about his own position. Again, before the entry
of July 1 in that year he inserts a similar paragraph of
"Observations". In subsequent years he puts any
general remarks on the year as a whole, if he makes
any, into the last entry of the previous year; and on
June 30 in 1663 and 1665 when he comes to the end
of a volume he makes a similar general survey of his
position and of public events.

There is nothing therefore in the seemingly intro-
ductory passage at the beginning to point to the
first volume as we have it being indisputably the first
volume or first year of diary he ever wrote. On the
other hand, the way in which he at once appears to
be so comfortably at home in diary writing and uses
shorthand seems rather to point to a previous attempt,
perhaps in longhand, which he destroyed when the
pages were bound up together. The entry on March 9,
1669, in which he speaks of having kept a diary "these
eight or ten years" does not absolutely preclude such
a possibility. The marvellous neatness of the writing
leads to the idea of the Diary having been copied out
by Pepys, who may not have begun again at the
very beginning.

We must remember that he had been successfully

cut for the stone in the previous year on March 26, 1658/59. He must have been laid up for several months recovering from the operation. It is not unlikely that during these months with ample time for reflection it occurred to Pepys that he would keep a diary. Although he was at that time only a clerk to George Downing, one of the Tellers of the Receipt of the Exchequer, his patron, Sir Edward Montagu, afterwards Lord Sandwich, had already befriended him, his finances had improved: "my own private condition very handsome", he says, and consequently he felt himself to be a man with certain prospects who might come into touch with events worth recording in a diary.

Yet another conjecture may be ventured: Pepys may have begun his Diary before his illness and operation. Weeks during which it was impossible for him to write left a considerable blank in the pages but did not prevent him from resuming methodically on January 1 following. In arranging the Diary for the binder he put aside the entries of the broken interval before his operation so as to have a completely consecutive record.

These conjectures are not entirely fanciful, because on the whole adult diarists more often than not make some remark by way of explanation, preface, or intention when they embark on diary writing, and many go so far as to summarise their lives from their birth up to the date of writing.

At any rate the resolution to write if not the beginning of the Diary must have been made some time before January 1. Pepys was not a man of impetuous habits who would suddenly seize a book and begin to scribble. We may be sure the book was purchased for the purpose some time beforehand. On the whole, therefore, it would not be surprising if some entries in longhand or even in shorthand were attempted and subsequently destroyed before he settled down into his carefully written shorthand. The first octavo-sized volume proved to be too small. The subsequent volumes are almost quarto size.

There are other instances of shorthand in diaries, such, for instance, as Byrom's diary already referred to, and the diary kept by John Russell, the eighteenth-century pastel artist. If secrecy is required, cipher also is very often used; and there are cases of German or Greek characters being adopted for purposes of concealment. This is obviously convenient, as a diarist can leave his book about without fear of its being read. Foreign languages are not uncommon. When John Richards, a Dorsetshire squire who lived in the days of William III., made references of a rather acrimonious nature about his wife in his diary he always broke into Italian. John Baker, a Sussex solicitor, was fond of this device for no particular reason. He uses, for instance, four languages in the very innocent entry, "*Uxor* went *hier* in chaise *con* little Patty". Pepys uses three languages when less innocently he writes: "There left her *sans essayer alcune cose con elle*". But he also uses this curious jargon on occasions when, just as in the case of Baker, there seems no need for concealment: "We did *biber* a good deal *de vino et je* did give *elle* twelve *soldi para comprare elle* some *gans* for a new *anno's* gift". We can see him giggling as he wrote this.

So far as the shorthand is concerned we are inclined to think that Pepys used it as a convenience much more than as a secret cipher. The Tangier Journal

was also written in shorthand and in that there was
nothing whatever which he could want to conceal.
He evidently wrote shorthand very easily and it therefore enabled him to write quickly. His writing
consequently is like someone talking. This is one of
the chief merits of his style. Of his use of cipher and
foreign languages a word will be said later.

There is no question that Pepys did not want his
contemporaries, and especially his wife, to read his
Diary, and shorthand therefore may have been some
safeguard. But further he did not even want anyone
to know he had written it. He was not like the diarist
who reads out his or her diary to an admiring circle of
friends. When he finds that Sir William Coventry
keeps a journal of "the material things", he tells him
that he also keeps one; "and he is the only man I ever
told it to, I think, that I kept it most strictly these
eight or ten years; and I am sorry almost that I told
him, it not being necessary, nor may be convenient to
have it known".

If Pepys wrote indecent and obscene passages in
his Diary, he by no means stands alone among diarists.
Some of the passages not reproduced in the full edition
refer merely to illness, his own or his wife's. Health
has a very strong influence over a conscientious daily
writer, far more than over a writer who summarises
periods. The pain or discomfort experienced very
naturally affects his mood on the day he writes. The
more regular the diarist the more often are his entries
interspersed with some account of his physical ailments.
John Baker, already mentioned, elaborated them into
medical treatises. James Clegg, an eighteenth-century
minister who "practiced physick", makes a special

point of diseases and cures, and many other diarists
have given intimate details. Pepys put down his own
and his wife's passing ailments in plain, unadorned, and
quite unscientific language, which of course is not fit
for reproduction.

Two further characteristics may be found in the
manuscript pages of private diaries before the editor's
blue pencil, too often ruthlessly used, has begun its
work. The first is the confession of discreditable
faults. Consciousness of failure, vice, sin, call it what
you will, prompts a diarist to write. It is the private
exercise of the instinct of confession. The diary acts
as a confidant. But the fear of a possible reader's eye
forces on him a sort of reticence which permits him
only to hint and insinuate, but not to describe. The
murderer, the poisoner, the thief, and the forger,
should they keep diaries, will not make confessions of
intention or performance. On the contrary, they are
dishonest enough, as in the case of the two poisoners
Palmer and Pritchard, to use their diary as a screen
to put people off the scent. Fortunately only a small
minority of human beings are addicted to actual crime.
The faults which beset us all, selfishness, conceit,
meanness, cupidity, dishonesty, etc., are seldom confessed, because they are not recognised, and because
they are not necessarily evident on any particular
occasion or on any particular day. The diarist who
makes self-analytical surveys may sometimes deplore
his tendency to certain of these defects, but it will be
in more or less general terms. Dr. Rutty's recitals of
instances of his greed and bad temper are unique.
Several diarists record their lapses with regard to drink.
But for the most part they are very reluctant to write

down in black and white facts and experiences on account of which posterity would certainly condemn them.

There is, however, a type of weakness, private and secret, which, like drink, culminates in quite specific and recognisable thoughts and actions, and which therefore claims the constant and special attention of diarists. Sensual aberrations and sexual misdeeds have been scored out of diaries by editors' pencils more than any other type of secret entry. No fault is more common and no weakness displays more acutely the double nature of all men. Times without number in diaries it is hinted at as "my wickedness", "my foulness", "my uncleanness", "my vileness", etc. But instances might be mentioned of descriptive passages occurring in the diaries of highly venerated and otherwise spiritually minded men who have felt impelled by what may seem almost mental alienation to record at length such experiences both normal and perverted. No one should blame them for the mental or physical experience of sexual extravagances except those who can claim that their entirely passionless nature has rendered their mind refined beyond blemish. But many will marvel at their writing it all down.

This brings us to the second and far more curious impulse. It takes the form of writing down obscenities, partly from the low pleasure of recalling discreditable experiences, and partly from an impulse to give vent to a suppressed and consequently strong and even morbid sensuality. A diary, of course, is not the only medium for this strange practice. The pathological phenomenon of seemingly innocent and exemplary people using under delirium foul and obscene language is by no means uncommon. That pleasure should be found in writing down privately such descriptions, whether imagined or experienced, may be distressing, but it is not abnormal.

Now, so far as confessions are concerned, Pepys shows little remorse in his escapades, and it is certain that he did not describe them for disciplinary purposes of self-correction. While he no doubt experienced some pleasure in recalling his shameless indecencies, there is no inclination on his part to expatiate on them in the vein of a victim of suppressed erotomania. In rapidly surveying his day the incidents naturally stand out in relief. They are therefore recorded faithfully with all the rest, quite incidentally, not in any way dominating the other happenings of the day, but falling into their place. While he is never thinking of any eye of a reader, his pen nevertheless sometimes, although not always, hesitates to write down the crude word or phrase, so he scribbles it in French or Spanish or in quite easily decipherable hieroglyphics. This is not concealment; it is, so to speak, the shyness of the cool recorder who, for the moment at any rate, does not share the lust of his other errant self. If he is in the mood which gloats and chuckles, down it goes in plain English. That he was inwardly a coarse-minded sensualist may be true; although he often shows that he is by no means incorrigibly dissolute, and has a certain, perhaps capricious, standard of his own, which at moments appears almost puritanical—as, for example, when he writes "God forgive me" because he was stringing his lute on a Sunday. But the point we are concerned with here is that the occurrence of these passages principally serves to show the meticulous completeness of his diary

writing, its absolute candour, and that never for a
moment did he imagine anyone reading his record.
In fact the impropriety of certain passages is more
important as showing Pepys's honesty as a diarist than
as a proof of the coarseness of his disposition. Considering the sort of society he knew and lived in,
and the constantly discussed dissipation of the Court
in Restoration days, it is indeed surprising that he
does not relate more bawdy stories and objectionable
incidents.

We are therefore presented with this curious psychological problem in these candid confessions of his gross
misdemeanours and callous infidelities. Outwardly
Pepys played the part of a dignified official and a
respected patron of the arts. There is nothing in our
first seventeenth-century portrait of him to lead us to
suppose that he failed in any way to give this impression. Yet daily in his diary he went out of his way to
expose a very different nature. As R. L. Stevenson
says, "It seems he has no design but to appear
respectable and here he keeps a private book to prove
he was not"—and, we may add, makes no sort of
provision for its destruction. There is no other diary
in which so marked a difference between the outward
and inward man has come to light.

Never can it be said more truly of any diarist that he
had no reader's eye in view. However, when he sorts
his papers and destroys many of them he does not
touch the Diary. No special instructions were left
with regard to it except that it was eventually included
in the Pepysian library. But in the long and elaborate
injunctions with regard to the library the volumes of the
Diary are never separately mentioned; although every

time he recatalogued his library (which occurred at least half a dozen times) the Diary volumes were handled by him and given fresh numbers, as their fly-leaves now show.

The absence of instructions with regard to a diary is far more common than either instructions to destroy or instructions to publish. The great majority of diarists just leave their record without a word of guidance to their immediate successors. When in their most destructive mood, convinced perhaps of their own insignificance, they may throw papers, letters, nay, deeds and wills into the fire, but something makes them hesitate when their hand stretches out to the series of their diary volumes. Their destruction is an amputation they cannot face; the diary is part of themselves with the life still in it. They seem to realise that they themselves cannot possibly judge of the merits of what they have written. So diaries escape; they survive with the writer's motive in leaving them undisclosed.

Pepys did not re-read his Diary. With the exception of an unimportant addition of dates of death to a list of names (written in longhand as all names were) there are no corrections, additions, or alterations. It seems clear that he had not the weakness common to so many diarists of reading over his past effusions, although this may be attributed to his failing eyesight. Writing shorthand is one thing, re-reading it easily would in any case be a labour.

The Diary contained notes which might be useful to him in future. He had many such notes in his Naval Minutes which, as it turned out, he never used. He forgot, perhaps, how full and indiscreet the Diary was, but it is certain that he had no conception whatever of the value of what he had written.

Pepys wrote practically daily with very few broken intervals. He sometimes wrote on separate sheets and then copied them out afterwards. The merit of a diary rests very largely on impressions of the day written freshly on the day. Parson Woodforde, whose excellent diary has recently been made available, gives us a valuable picture of village life in the eighteenth century, not by his reflections nor by disquisitions on public and social events, but by very regular and careful daily writing of the small domestic affairs which came immediately under his notice. Daily writing by one who knows not what the morrow will bring endows a diary with a vivid reflection of life's uncertainty and gives it the very element which cannot be found in any other form of writing.

Pepys wrote for rather over nine years and only left off because of his eyesight:

Being not able to do it any longer, having done now so long as to undo my eyes almost every time that I take a pen in my hand.

In the learned treatises on Pepys's eyesight the following entry in his Diary appears to have been overlooked; it was written on board the *Naseby* before Charles II. came on board:

The gun over against my cabbin I fired myself to the king, which was the first time he had been saluted by his own ships since this change, but holding my head too much over the gun, I had almost spoiled my right eye.

It is more than probable that this accident was the cause of his trouble with his eyes in later years. Many regret that Pepys ceased writing. Coleridge thought it was "a greater and more grievous loss to the mind's eye of posterity than to the bodily organs of Pepys himself". This is no doubt true. But we may console ourselves that it is often better to have too little of a good thing than to run the risk of a deterioration in quality by having more.

The Tangier Journal he did not include in his collection of books. He kept this journal for three months in 1683—that is to say, fourteen years after he left off writing his Diary. It is almost exclusively official. He was an older man, no doubt a soberer, wiser, and more cautious man, but he certainly was a very much less good diarist. We can only just recognise him by one or two touches of personal detail. But his official judgements about the work in hand are unexceptionable and show us the Secretary of the Admiralty as altogether a more staid, solemn, and responsible person than the Clerk of the Acts. There is a hint of our old friend in an entry where he states he has been writing letters home, "among others a merry, roguish yet mysterious one to S. H.".

But to return to the main Diary: what are the chief merits which give it its unique position among all diaries? First and foremost, Pepys did not write for disciplinary reasons nor, as has been noted, for any special reader. He wrote because he enjoyed writing. In this he resembles another very eminent diarist, Sir Walter Scott. Not till he was fifty-six did Scott begin "journalizing", but the obvious enjoyment with which he wrote is the very element which makes his journal such delightful reading. "I am enamoured of my journal," he says, and again, "I think this journal will suit me well".

G

Nothing is more difficult than the comparison of diaries. Depending as they do on the individuality of the writer, they may be good for very different reasons. A fault in one may amount almost to a merit in another where the treatment is slightly different. Introspection, for instance, can be irritating when it is accompanied by excessive self-depreciation, yet the introspective note is what makes diaries like those of Marie Bash-kirtseff and Barbellion specially interesting. Even these, however, are self-conscious and lacking in honesty. Pepys was not introspective and therefore does not suffer from these faults. Amiel was scientific in his self-analysis and quite honest, but no one reads Amiel's journal for entertainment. In the haze of his abnormal analytical self-dissection the atmosphere of his private life is smothered. Learning does not improve a diary. In spite of Evelyn's scholarship his Diary is on a very much lower level than that of his friend. This is partly due to his having written it up and epitomised periods. One feels that he registers only what he wanted to be known publicly. It would be interesting to know if in the course of their conversation together either of them had suggested to the other that diary writing was a desirable habit.

Fanny Burney's power of narration is of a higher order than that of Pepys and her capacity of reporting conversations unequalled. But the writer of fiction too often gets the upper hand over the recorder of facts and in the latter part of her diary she becomes diffuse and long-winded. Charles Greville, also an official, confines himself very nearly exclusively to a record of the political history of his day, and, important as his journal is, the colour of individuality is comparatively

faint. On the other hand, Benjamin Haydon's diary,
one of the most remarkable of English diaries, is
charged with his personality. He carries his reader
along in amusement at his unrestrained tirades and
violent polemics and in amazement at his brilliant
pen-portraits of his contemporaries. Known to his
friends as a bad painter, a mad eccentric, and an
importunate beggar, he was discovered by posterity
to be in the midst of all his craziness a very shrewd
observer and skilful recorder of the events of his life.
But his egotism is excessive, his invective tiring, and
his supplications unreadable. The long diary of Lord
Shaftesbury gives the man's full life-story; his public
spirit and his austerity penetrate in almost every
entry. Full and honest as it is, there is no light touch,
no entertainment, no observation of the trivialities
which give colour and ornament to life, and it is
therefore difficult to read. In a lighter vein is Tom
Moore's diary. But his pleasant intimate gossip was
written for publication.

In some of the diaries of more obscure people we
find elements of naïveté and charm which are lacking
in the records of those who have had to deal with
greater events and have lived among eminent people.
Thomas Turner, the Sussex storekeeper, and William
Jones, the Vicar of Broxbourne, had special *flair* for
diary writing. We get personality and atmosphere,
spontaneity and humour unspoiled by any intention
of publication. Dr. Edward Dale's few entries of
Court life and descriptions of the Princesses Mary and
Anne (afterwards Queens) are too scrappy to merit very
much attention, but he undoubtedly had something of
the Pepysian touch in his gossip. Swift has a witty

sparkle, and Byron in his brief attempts an amusing, indiscreet recklessness. Both, however, had readers in view. There is a suggestion of playing to the gallery. In humour and certainly in candour Pepys is their superior.

Pepys in fact can hold his own and surpass all diarists by merits which some of the others have and by merits which none of the others have. As already pointed out, he was a regular daily writer and his impressions are therefore fresh; his candour is a proof of his honesty, and he had no thought of publication. The genius appears in his power of selecting the incidents and epitomising situations, in the casual jotting of humorous opinions, the marvellous observation of intriguing situations, the restraint in handling the larger events, and the delicacy in which he can lighten them by a whimsical word or phrase, the keen enjoyment in which he reports his good fortune, the optimism and joy which always chases away the gloom of despondency, and the introduction of the intimate, the secret, nay, even the obscene in their proper place with disarming ingenuousness. We laugh with him, we laugh at him, and we are always entertained.

Whether Pepys was moral, scrupulous, learned, or clever has nothing whatever to do with the excellence of his Diary. We find all this out when we read it because he tells us everything.

A full and sincere diary is to some extent a revelation. It may be the revelation of expected and characteristic thoughts and opinions; it may be the revelation of unsuspected thoughts and deeds; it may also be the revelation of hitherto unknown qualities, the fact of them being unknown redounding very much to the credit of the diarist. Because of its completeness Pepy's Diary is too often judged, so far as he personally is concerned, as a revelation of the weaknesses and moral lapses which were not observed by his contemporaries. But in order to be fair, this nosing out of unsavoury passages and chuckling over his follies and faults must be balanced by the observation of excellent qualities to which he only refers incidentally. He may have been timid and nervous physically: several occasions on which he was frightened are entered perfectly honestly. But in the far more important sphere of moral courage and in kindness to the unfortunate he is shown up in the Diary in a very favourable light. For instance when Lord Brouncker, who was no favourite with Pepys, fell into disfavour, Pepys walked with him in Westminster Hall although he "was almost troubled to be seen" with him. He considered him wrongly accused, and declares he is "able to justify him in all that he is under so much scandal for". It was a bold act for a subordinate official to send "a great letter of reproof" to his chief. When Pepys sent his well-reasoned but severe letter to Lord Sandwich on November 18, 1663, he confesses he is "afeard of what the consequences may be". But in discharging what he considered to be an important public duty he had no hesitation.

Again in 1669, when there was question of dismissing officers of the Navy, Pepys writes:

I have not a mind indeed at this time to be put out of my office if I can make shift that is honourable to keep it; but I will not do it by deserting the Duke of York.

When his cousin Joyce drowned himself Pepys quite unostentatiously took very great trouble to help his widow. He goes and comforts her, "though I can find she can, as all other women, cry, and yet talk of other things all in a breath". At a time when he was under grave suspicion of being a Roman Catholic he almost quixotically invited Cesare Morelli the singer to stay with him as his guest, although Morelli's membership of the Church of Rome told against the Secretary of the Admiralty, who was accused of harbouring a priest.

Other instances could be found, but they must be searched for, because they are never stressed. Pepys was incapable of writing for effect. When he was moved his rapid shorthand correctly conveys his emotion. The description of Sir Christopher Mings's funeral which he attended with Sir W. Coventry is very striking. He gives verbatim the tribute paid to their dead commander by "a dozen able, lusty, proper men" who came to their coach side; and then he adds his own:

Sir Christopher Mings was a very stout man, and a man of great parts and most excellent tongue among ordinary men. . . . He had brought his family into a way of being great; but dying at this time, his memory and name will be quite forgot in a few months as if it had never been, nor any of his name be the better for it; he having not had time to will any estate, but is dead poor rather than rich.

The self-conscious writer would have ended there, saying to himself, "I won't spoil that by recording anything else to-day". But Pepys went on. He reports a far from innocent visit to Mrs. Bagwell, and ends up his entry, "In my way home I called on a fisherman and bought three eeles which cost me three shillings". Is it too much to say that the value of what is serious when it occurs is greatly enhanced by a writer who also can admit his incorrigible frivolity?

A sentence in an entry can be very eloquent. An entry of pages may tell you nothing. The length of Pepys's entries varies according to his mood; unlike the over-methodical diarist, he does not confine his report of the day's doings to an equally measured space of page. He writes at some length when in the vein and when events prompt him. But even his short entries reflect his mood and are wonderfully informing. Here is the brief and very comprehensive record of April 10, 1668:

All the morning at Office. At noon with W. Pen, to Duke of York and attended Council. So to Duck Lane and there kissed bookseller's wife and bought legend. So home, coach, Sailor. Mrs Hannam dead. News of peace. Conning my gamut.

Pepys reflects his mood by the length or brevity of his entries and by the style of his narrative rather than by any deliberate confessions of depression or elation. Often we can picture him writing as when he tells us the candle is going out, "which makes me write thus slobberingly". Or again: "I staid up till the bellman came by with his bell under my window, as I was writing of this very line, and cried 'Past one of the clock, and a cold, frosty, windy morning'"; and could the suggestion of depression be better indicated than it is by the simple word "and" in the concluding sentence on October 9, 1664? "To bed without prayers it being cold and to-morrow washing day."

When he writes at length he is never wearisome. His Sunday outing on Epsom Downs on July 14, 1667, is described at great length. This was purely because

he enjoyed it so much, not because anything of importance occurred. As it is one of the prettiest passages
in the Diary, and as it shows us Pepys not as an official
nor as a frivolous townsman, but as an appreciator of
simple beauty, a couple of extracts may be given:

. . . the women and W. Hewer and I walked upon the
Downes where a flock of sheep was; and the most pleasant
and innocent sight that ever I saw in my life—we find a
shepherd and his little boy reading, far from any houses
or sight of people, the Bible to him; so I made the boy read
to me which he did with the forced tone that childern do
usually read, that was mighty pretty, and then I did give
him something, and went to the father and talked with him;
and I find he had been a servant in my cozen Pepys's house,
and told me what was become of their own servants. He
did content himself mightily in my liking his boy's reading,
and did bless God for him, the most like one of the old
patriarchs that ever I saw in my life and it brought those
thoughts of the old age of the world in my mind for two or
three days after. We took notice of his woolen stockings of
two colours mixed and of his shoes shod with iron shoes
both at the toe and heels and with great nails in the soles
of his feet which was mighty pretty.

. . . took coach, it being about seven at night, and
passed and saw the people walking with their wives and
childern to take the ayre, and we set out for home, the
sun by and by going down, and we in the cool of the
evening all the way with much pleasure home talking and
pleasing ourselves with the pleasure of this day's work. . . .
Anon it grew dark, and as it grew dark we had the pleasure
to see several glow-worms which was mighty pretty.

A close scrutiniser of diaries will find words in the
earlier part of this entry which show that it was not
written on the day. They are the words, "for two or
three days after". The next two entries are un-
questionably written on the day and the explanation

comes on the third day, when he writes that he goes to his chamber "to set down my Journall of Sunday last with much pleasure". This shows—and there may be other occasions which cannot so easily be detected—that when he had something very special he reserved the writing of it for a time when he had plenty of leisure, going on meanwhile with the ordinary daily entries.

Another excellent long description of an entirely different scene is the entry on January 1, 1667/68, in which he minutely pictures a gambling scene at "the Groome-Porter's", where all the different types of people and different manners of winning and losing are described. As it is not an entry which is often quoted and yet contains examples both of his powers of observation and his peculiar aptitude for succinct expression, a section of it may be given in full.

. . . they begun to play at about eight at night, where to see how differently one man took his losing from another, one cursing and swearing, and another only muttering and grumbling to himself, a third without any apparent discontent at all; to see how the dice will run good luck in one hand, for half an hour together, and another have no good luck at all; to see how easily here, where they play nothing but guinnys, a £100 is won or lost; to see two or three gentlemen come in there drunk, and putting their stock of gold together, one 22 pieces, the second 4, and the third 5 pieces; and these to play one with another, and forget how much each of them brought, but he that brought the 22 thinks that he brought no more than the rest; to see the different humours of gamesters to change their luck, when it is bad, how ceremonious they are as to call for new dice, to shift their places, to alter their manner of throwing, and that with great industry, as if there was anything in it; to see how some old gamesters, that have no money now to spend as formerly, do come and sit and look on, as among others, Sir Lewis Dives, who was here, and hath been a great gamester in his time; to hear their cursing and damning to no purpose, as one man being to throw a seven if he could, and, failing to do it after a great many throws, cried he would be damned if ever he flung seven more while he lived, his despair of throwing it being so great, while others did it as their luck served almost every throw; to see how persons of the best quality do here sit down, and play with people of any, though meaner; and to see how people in ordinary clothes shall come hither, and play away 100, or 2 or 300 guinnys, without any kind of difficulty; and lastly, to see the formality of the groome-porter, who is their judge of all disputes in play and all quarrels that may arise therein, and how his under-officers are there to observe true play at each table, and to give new dice, is a consideration I never could have thought had been in the world, had I not now seen it. And mighty glad I am that I did see it, and it may be will find another evening, before Christmas is over, to see it again, when I may stay later, for their heat of play begins not till about eleven or twelve o'clock; which did give me another pretty observation of a man, that did win mighty fast when I was there. I think he won £100 at single pieces in a little time. While all the rest envied him his good fortune, he cursed it, saying, ' A pox on it, that it should come so early upon me, for this fortune two hours hence would be worth something to me, but then, God damn me, I shall have no such luck '. This kind of prophane, mad entertainment they give themselves. And so I, having enough for once, refusing to venture, though Brisband pressed me hard, and tempted me with saying that no man was ever known to lose the first time, the devil being too cunning to discourage a gamester; and he offered me also to lend me ten pieces to venture; but I did refuse, and so went away, and took coach and home about 9 or 10 at night.

While the noting of trivialities gives colour to a diary, they can be and are in the case of some diaries insignificant and pointless. With Pepys the trivial note nearly

always gives spice and character to his entry. When
he meets Sir J. Lawson and has a very short talk with
him, this would appear to be an incident not worth
recording. But Pepys gives us the reason, "his hickup
not being gone could have little discourse with him".

The Diary has suffered, as was inevitable, from the
extraction of plums, the quotation of snippets, and the
abbreviation of entries. Those who have read the full
version are better able to judge the painstaking and
methodical industry of the man. The full flavour and
humanity of a diary can only be appreciated by reading
consecutive entries, even though some of them may
be devoid of historical interest or even of individual
peculiarities. His meticulous recital of the seemingly
unimportant has to be studied daily in order that the
living man may be clearly discerned. But it is important to remember in attempting to estimate the
man from the pages of his Diary that we can only
examine nine and a half years of the seventy that
he lived.

The entries contain no long philosophic or even
political disquisitions—just a skilful recital of events.
There are no elaborate character sketches with biographical details, but he hits off people in two or three
lines certainly without a moment's hesitation as he
wrote. A few of these passing comments may be
quoted.

(Major Waters); a deaf and most amorous melancholy
gentleman who is under a despayr in love . . . which
makes him bad company though a most good natured man.

(Aunt James); a poor religious well meaning, good soul
talking of nothing but God Almighty and that with so much
innocence that mightily pleased me.

(Mr. Case); a dull fellow in his talk and all in the Presbyterian manner; a great deal of noise and a kind of religious tone but very dull.

(Mrs. Horsefield); one of the veriest citizen's wives in the world, so full of little silly talk and now and then a little sillily bawdy.

One can learn a great deal about a man from his observation of other people. Three of these descriptions taken at random from among the many show that he was pleased with simplicity, intolerant of pomposity, and put off by pretentious coarseness. Many fine shades of character may be detected in diary entries always provided that the writer is spontaneous and not consciously describing himself.

Perhaps Pepys's style is not what is called literary; his grammar may be faulty—it often is—his phrasing clumsy. All this does not matter in the smallest degree in diary writing. There are excellent diaries in which phrasing, and even grammar, spelling, and punctuation are all execrable. Charles Russell (1898), a foreman riveter, shows in an unpublished diary that he had no conception of grammar or of spelling, but his lively narrative of his adventures in Africa could not be improved. Your literary man who thinks about his English, his style, his balance, and his epigrams is very unlikely to be a good diarist. There are indeed not many literary men even who are capable of the terse powers of lucid expression sometimes displayed by Pepys. Without sententious epigram he can epitomise an event, a situation, or a character in phrases which would be spoilt by the alteration of a single word. Mother wit often counts more than education.

If diaries are to be classed as literature—and they most certainly ought to be—we must in considering them broaden our judgements and canons of taste with regard to style.

When a man can give you a vivid picture of events and personalities and convey to you his sense of living through his life with all his passing hopes and misgivings, joys and sorrows, petty irritations and high aspirations, and at the same time never weary you but invariably entertain you, his style must have some supreme merit however much it may violate the orthodox standards to which writers are supposed to conform.

There is sometimes a tendency to adopt towards the Diary an attitude of patronising amusement, to regard it merely as the effusions of an entertaining scribbler. Such critics seem to suggest that we could all write diaries of this sort if we wanted to or if we tried, and that after a couple of hundred years our records would be read with as much interest and amusement as we find in reading Pepys.

Let anyone try! Many have tried within the last two or three hundred years, and how few in their efforts come within any measurable distance of comparison with Pepys! To write regularly requires discipline. Not all are capable of this to begin with. Always to feel inclination requires a peculiar sort of effort. To epitomise your day so as to give a true picture of it requires special discrimination and power of selection. By powers of selection we mean the choice of incident. A mere recital of consecutive incidents is not enough. Certain thoughts and deeds must be detached which may be trivial and not immediately relevant, but they may reflect the outward atmosphere and inward mood and make a reader feel present. This requires skill. After all, every minute of everyone's day is filled. Strother, the York shop assistant, endeavoured to write down *everything* that happened in the day. Of course it was impossible, and he gave up the attempt after two or three days. A sentence or two would have given him in his old age just as vivid an impression of those days as his laborious and almost unreadable effort. But selection, which is perhaps the most important element in a diarist's outfit, cannot be learned. No hard work, preparation, or study will make a man into a good diarist. It is not a matter of conforming to recognised standards. There are none. A good diarist *nascitur non fit*. There is no question of taking advice or of thinking out and culti-vating an ingenious method. It all rests with the attitude of mind, the disposition and the instinctive inclination of the writer. Although almost every effort at diary writing has peculiar interest, success depends more on temperament than equipment.

On the other hand, the opposite tendency to regard Pepys as an outstanding extraordinary man and a great wit and observer is equally wide of the mark. As the earlier chapters have shown, he was quite an ordinary man, in no other way exceptionally talented, and as a writer in the literary sense he may quite justifiably be rather severely criticised.

Yet another opinion put forward by those who rightly appreciated Pepys's official pre-eminence is that the Diary is a "by-product" of no particular account; that there is nothing remarkable about his writing the Diary, that his claim to fame is that he was the "right hand of the Navy", and that such a man should write such a Diary if anything detracts from his greatness. There have, however, been many equally admirable, and indeed more admirable, Civil Servants than Pepys whose names are forgotten, whereas in his capacity as a diarist he stands alone. That official work is infinitely more important than writing a diary is a contention that need not be disputed. However, to be merely noteworthy in the one but supreme in the other alters the balance of the comparison.

But in all of these views the central point of interest is missed, a point which is perhaps more psychological than intellectual or literary. It is that an average man, inconspicuous and, although assiduous in his work, by no means specially gifted, should have been able, unsuspected by his contemporaries and even by himself, to have perpetrated a work of undoubted genius in a realm which about twenty-five per cent of educated people have privately explored without, except in a very few instances, approaching anywhere near the same result.

So much has been said of the side-lights thrown by Pepys on the events of his day, on the manners, customs, and fashions, and on his own domestic life. But too little has been said of the unsurpassed efficacy of the method in diary writing which his genius adopted and of his temperamental fitness for this self-imposed task.

Pepys's claim to be placed among Men of Letters must rest alone on the Diary. The remainder of his literary output is entirely negligible. The claim is well founded, and a by no means inferior position among the immortals has readily been accorded to him.

CHAPTER VI

THE OFFICIAL

THE task of the historian so well described by Evelyn is exceedingly laborious. He collects his documents and makes his survey, depending as he goes back into the past on fewer and fewer contemporary notices of the period he is studying. The day-to-day notes of an observer are of priceless value to him because they give the opinion of an actual spectator of the events, and are likely to supply personal touches and points of detail which will allow the historian to make his pictures far more realistic than if he had only to depend on official and public reports.

Many diarists have fallen into the error of filling their pages with accounts of public events which they themselves have not witnessed, but which they have seen described in news sheets. It may amuse them when they re-read their diaries to observe how they reacted to the great happenings of the day. But their observations are not of any sort of use to the historian.

Apart from the many diarists whose local and family references are of interest to a very restricted circle of people, there are few whose information throws a light on national history which could not be obtained from some other source. Sir Simonds d'Ewes has furnished a good deal of material for the history of the early Stewart period, Lord Egmont's punctilious record of parliamentary proceedings from 1728 onwards is so voluminous as to make up for the absence of any Hansard in those times. Fanny Burney on the Court of George III. is inimitable, and Wolfe Tone discloses the inner workings of his own great but mad adventure. Charles Greville is perhaps the most famous for revealing the inner side of the political events of his times, and in Scotland James Melville, although very early, endows the dry ecclesiastical controversies of the early seventeenth century with an astonishing amount of atmosphere by his first-hand accounts of disputes and his personal comments.

Pepys did not set out to be a historian. It happened that he was at the Admiralty at a time when the affairs of the Navy were very much to the fore, and was in a position not only to hear of matters of importance, but himself to help to shape events. From that point of vantage he came into touch with the greater lights who were the chief actors in the national drama. On the strictly official side there may be found in the *Admiralty Journal*,[1] which contains the minutes of the Admiralty Commission from January 1673 to April 1679, a very fine testimony to the business-like abilities of the Secretary of the Admiralty, who was responsible for keeping the minutes. The Journal contains a summary of debates as well as the conclusions reached, and the reports are examples of the orderly method and good sense of their compiler. But through the Diary the

---

[1] " Catalogue of the Pepysian Manuscripts ", vol. iv., *Admiralty Journal*, edited by J. R. Tanner.

non-expert reader may learn more of Pepys's activities as an official.

The vision of a diarist of course suffers from being too close to the events he records. His perspective therefore is faulty. Diary writing, moreover, is a bad medium for registering a sequence of events. There are repetitions, omissions, irrelevancies, and even contradictions which are apt to make a tangle that may sometimes be difficult to unravel. Nevertheless the impressions of the day's doings made on the day by one who has special facilities for his observations cannot fail to give history the element which it so often lacks, namely, a living spirit of actuality, the human note of things experienced.

Pepys's Diary fills in for us many blanks in the history of the early part of Charles II.'s reign. The particulars with regard to the naval preparations for the Dutch War, and his accounts of the Plague and the Fire of London are of the greatest value. Moreover, his passing comments on some of the leading characters of the day give fresh detail and in some cases modify the estimates we have made of them.

On naval matters we do not get the point of view of the ordinary man in the street, but of the official with all his doubts and misgivings. Short extracts from the Diary have illuminated the pages of so many books, and this of course can be done again and again.

Let us take a full entry in which the punctilious official, amazing diarist, and curious man records in 1666, on June 7, the facts which came to light with regard to the engagement with the Dutch after the premature rejoicing over a supposed victory. In recording the victory on the previous day Pepys tells us in an aside, "that which pleased me as much as the news was to have the fair Mrs. Middleton at our church, who indeed is a very beautiful lady". It will be noted that during the following day his occupations were not exclusively official.

Up betimes, and to my office about business (Sir W. Coventry having sent me word that he is gone down to the fleete to see how matters stand, and to be back again speedily); and with the same expectation of congratulating ourselves with the victory that I had yesterday. But my Lord Bruncker and Sir T. H. that come from Court, tell me quite contrary newes, which astonishes me; that is to say, that we are beaten, lost many ships and good commanders; have not taken one ship of the enemy's; and so can only report ourselves a victory; nor is it certain that we were left masters of the field. But, above all, that The Prince run on shore upon the Galloper, and there stuck; was endeavoured to be fetched off by the Dutch, but could not; and so they burned her; and Sir G. Ascue is taken prisoner, and carried into Holland. This newes do much trouble me, and the thoughts of the ill consequences of it, and the pride and presumption that brought us to it. At noon to the 'Change, and there find the discourse of towne, and their countenances much changed; but yet not very plain. So home to dinner, all alone, my father and people being gone all to Woolwich to see the launching of the new ship The Greenwich, built by Chr. Pett. I left alone with little Mrs. Tooker, whom I kept with me in my chamber all the afternoon, and did what I would with her. By and by comes Mr. Wayth to me; and discoursing of our ill successe, he tells me plainly from Captain Page's own mouth (who hath lost his arm in the fight) that the Dutch did pursue us two hours before they left us, and then they suffered us to go on homewards, and they retreated towards their coast; which is very sad newes. Then to my office and anon to White Hall, late to the Duke of York to see what commands he hath and to pray a meeting to-morrow for Tangier in behalf of Mr. Yeabsly, which I did do and do find the Duke much damped in his discourse, touching the late fight, and all the Court talk sadly of it. The Duke did give me several letters he had received from the fleete and Sir W. Coventry and Sir W. Pen, who are gone down thither, for me to pick out some works to be done for the setting out the fleete again; and so I took them home with me, and was drawing out an abstract of them till mid-night. And as to newes, I do find great reason to think that we are beaten in every respect, and that we are the losers. The Prince upon the Galloper, where both the Royall Charles and Royall Katherine had come twice aground, but got off. The Essex carried into Holland; the Swiftsure missing (Sir William Barkeley) ever since the beginning of the fight. Captains Bacon, Tearne, Wood, Mootham, Whitty, and Coppin slayne. The Duke of Albemarle writes, that he never fought with worse officers in his life, not above twenty of them behaving themselves like men. Sir William Clerke lost his leg; and in two days died. The Loyall George, Seven Oakes, and Swiftsure are still missing, having never as the Generall writes himself, engaged with them. I was as great an alteration to find myself required to write a sad letter instead of a triumphant one to my Lady Sandwich this night, as ever on any occasion I had in my life. So late home and to bed.

Pepys was not one of those officials for whom drafts and reports, parchments and red tape are the breath of their nostrils. He could not resist taking "great notice" of many other things. Lord Sandwich after a serious business talk with him "called for the fiddles and books and we two and W. Howe and Mr. Childe did sing and play some psalmes of Will Lawes's and some songs".

Nevertheless he was painstaking and conscientious down to the smallest detail. Even when copying he "takes great pleasure to rule the lines and have the capital words wrote with red ink". Although he stood out against the major forms of corruption he was not above making a bit for himself if he could manage it. On June 8, 1662, he writes:

At the office all the morning and dined at home and after dinner in all haste to make up my accounts with my Lord, which I did with some trouble, because I had some hopes to have made a profit to myself in this account and above what was due to me (which God forgive me in) but I could not, but carried them to my Lord with whom they passed well.

Yet just as we are condemning Pepys as frivolous and interested in many other things than his work we find in the complete honesty of his story that no one felt more keenly than he the humiliation of our defeat at the hands of the Dutch, and no one endeavoured more strenuously to devise remedies and to raise the necessary money to put the fleet in order. A student of Pepys cannot help being struck throughout that in connection with his official duties his judgement was good and his opinion was sound. Moreover, he never flinched from discharging disagreeable duties.

It must have required enormous courage for a subordinate official, as the Clerk of the Acts was, to confront the audience he faced on Sunday June 7, 1666. The Cabinet met in the Green Room at Whitehall. There were present the King, the Duke of York, Prince Rupert, Lord Chancellor, Lord Treasurer, Duke of Albemarle, Carteret, Coventry, and Morris. After they had assembled there was an embarrassing silence. But in this alarming interval it was the subordinate official, the Clerk of the Acts, who stood up, broke the silence, and made "a current and I thought a good speech, laying open the ill state of the navy". Prince Rupert was furious and spoke "in a heat". Another embarrassing silence, and Pepys withdrew with grave misgivings that the proceedings may "redound to my hurt". Coventry afterwards reassures him. But the point is that he makes no virtue of his courage and only shows genuine concern with regard to the Navy. How little known he was is shown in this entry by his saying "the Prince will be asking now who this Pepys is".

But no quotations of isolated passages can give the atmosphere of uncertainty, the controversies and factions, the apprehensions and misgivings like the consecutive reading of Pepys's full entries at this period, each of them relieved by the personal touches which show us the faulty and perhaps frivolous-minded writer fully aware of the crisis through which the country was passing, and very shrewdly detecting the causes.

The official was drawn into direct contact with the Court. As has been noted, he makes no deliberately drawn character sketches, but nevertheless his passing references threaded together give a very living picture even when they show a change in his own opinion. Take his estimate of Charles II.

When he first comes over, Pepys is favourably impressed. He records the King saying that the Bible "was the thing he loved above all things in the world". He describes him as "a very good natured man", and says he looked "most noble" and was "very kind to the Queen". But he hears and sees too much as time passes to keep up his good opinion, and gradually every reference to Charles becomes extremely critical, and he notes that the King's behaviour to the Queen "do give great discontent to all people". The official begins to see that his royal master takes no interest

whatever in the affairs of State. "The King do mind
nothing but pleasure and hates the very sight and
thoughts of business." "All I observed there [in the
Council Chamber] is the silliness of the King playing
with his dogs all the while and not minding business;
and what he said was mighty weak." "He speaks the
worst that ever I heard man in my life." Pepys talks
of his "horrid effeminacy", meaning love of women.
He sees him "coming privately from my Lady Castlemaine's; which is a poor thing for a Prince to do";
"The King do still doat on his women even beyond
all shame"; "the King is become besotted of Mrs.
Stewart"; "This lechery will never leave him";
"Nothing almost but bawdry at Court from top to
bottom". He is genuinely shocked at Charles's improper stories. He hears him and the Duke of York
making lewd remarks about the geese and ganders in
St. James's Park, "which did not please me" says our
moralist, and we know he means it because our own
experience is that however much humorous impropriety may appeal to us, we cannot stand it from certain
people. A bit of a snob himself, he condemns the
snobbish adulations of others. When he sees Charles
playing tennis he writes: "But to see how the King's
play was extolled without any cause at all, was a loath-
some sight, though sometimes indeed he did play very
well and deserved to be commended; but such open
flattery is beastly". He thinks it is to Charles's
"everlasting shame to have so idle a rogue" as
Rochester for his companion.

The King's and the Duke's drunken orgy together
is recorded with disapproval, and when his Majesty
climbs over a wall to visit the Duchess of Richmond,

Pepys calls it "a horrid shame". Violent invective against the King would not be so effective and would certainly be less genuine. That Evelyn should have denounced Charles and his Court is not surprising. But condemnation from Pepys who was easy-going and, as we know, by no means strait-laced, gives a stronger impression of the disgusting character of the Court atmosphere. Some of the unprintable passages occur in his remarks about the King.

Once, however, our musician official is pleased: "Here [in Whitehall Chapel] I first perceived that the King is a little musicall and kept good time with his hand all along the anthem". Passing snapshots like these are far better than a studio portrait. When the King thanks Pepys personally for his services after the Plague year, it is noted in the Diary that "he grasped me very kindly by the hand", but there is nothing about being "mightily pleased" or "to my great content". Evelyn was similarly treated the following day, and notes in his Diary the King's "most gracious manner". Charles knew well enough that by a word a King can get round most people.

But if Pepys was critical, as he undoubtedly was of most of the public men he came across, there is a very notable exception in the case of Sir William Coventry. In contrast to the above references to the King, we may adopt the same method and note his snapshots of Coventry. It will be remembered that Coventry was Secretary to the Duke of York, a notable Parliamentarian, and the most courageous and zealous of the Commissioners of the Navy. No life of him has been written, but there is no question that he was a man of very conspicuous ability, of excellent judgement, and,

for those times, exceptionally disinterested purpose.
That he should not have risen to a high position was
partly owing to his own lack of personal ambition, but
it more specially illustrates the disregard of the Restoration Court for real ability and its preference for second-
rate royal favourites. Charles II. may have been a
personally charming, picturesque, and amusing man,
but far too great a leniency is shown towards his
scandalous disregard for the nation's welfare, his
inexcusable ignorance of public affairs, and his preference for the company not only of disreputable but of
stupid people.

The highest commendation that can be given to
Pepys as an official is the fact that Coventry so greatly
valued his services. It is also very greatly to Pepys's
credit that he appreciated so warmly the character and
abilities of this remarkable man, for he is as a rule far
more lavish in his criticism than in his praise. In
contrast to his regard for Coventry, he positively
detested Sir William Penn, the distinguished commander, who was one of the Navy Board. He refers
to him as an "asse", "a coxcomb", "a false
knave", "a perfidious rogue", and when Pepys dines
with him he has "bad nasty supper, which makes
me not love the family". But let us hear Pepys on
Coventry.

At first he listens to the gossip against Coventry
that he "had already feathered his nest by the selling
of places", but he soon finds he must depend on him
to bring things "to a good condition in the office".
The intimacy grows, they walk and talk together, and
Pepys finds "most excellent discourse from him", and
Coventry on his side tells Lord Sandwich that Pepys

was "the life of this office". Two of Coventry's rules
are quoted:

> (1) of suspecting every man that proposes anything to
> him to be a knave; or at least to have some ends
> of his own in it.

> (2) that a man who cannot sit still in his chamber and
> he that cannot say no is not for business.

"The last of which", adds the Clerk of the Acts, "is a
great fault of mine which I must amend in."

Our diarist is not seeking anyone's praise as he
writes; we can therefore well believe him when he
reports that Sir William Coventry "do tell me so freely
his love and value of me", and as they talk over office
matters he finds him "to admiration good and industrious". He relates how Coventry tells him—

> He is resolved to try and never baulke taking notice of
> anything that is to the King's prejudice, let it fall where it
> will, which is a most brave resolution. He was very free
> with me; and by my troth, I do see more reall worth in
> him than in most men that I do know.

When Coventry proposes himself to dinner he is
tremendously proud, "but my dinner being a legg of
mutton and two capons, they were not done enough
which did vex me". Mrs. Pepys catches it afterwards.

It was Coventry's encouragement that made Pepys
think of writing a history of the Navy, a suggestion
which he says "sorts mightily with my genius". But
this friendship placed the subordinate official in an
awkward situation, because Lord Sandwich regarded
Coventry as "his greatest obstacle".

> Lord to see in what difficulty I stand that I dare not
> walk with Sir William Coventry for fear my Lord or Sir
> G. Carteret should see me; nor with either of them for fear
> Sir W. Coventry should.

In 1665 there is a touch of misgiving in an entry:

I observing with a little trouble that he is too great now to expect too much familiarity with and I find he do not mind me as he used to, but when I reflect upon him and his business I cannot think much of it for I do not observe anything but the same great kindness from him.

How well one can picture the humble official fearing that the great man is soaring out of his reach! But with what generosity and understanding does Pepys explain it! The following year, 1666, there is a note of awe in the entry:

. . . he being the activist man in the world and we all (myself particularly) more afeared of him than of the King or his service, for aught I see.

Then comes Coventry's fall. In March 1668/69 he is sent to the Tower.

. . . the King will never have a good counsellor, nor the Duke of York any sure friend to stick to him; nor any good man will be left to advise what is good. This, therefore, do heartily trouble me as anything that ever I heard.

Pepys goes to see him constantly at the Tower, and has long talks with him "to my great content". It was on one of these occasions that his confession with regard to keeping a diary was made. "All must go to rack", he reflects after one of his visits, "if the King do not come to see the want of such a servant". Even after Coventry's release the King refuses to let him kiss his hand. But Coventry did not repine at the loss of Court favour. He continued to take an active part in the House of Commons debates until the dissolution of 1678–79, when he retired into the country.

The references are of course fuller and more de-

tailed than the few sentences for which space can be
found here. They serve to show Pepys's perspicacity
and good judgement of character, and make us believe
that Coventry was not exaggerating when he said of
Pepys "it would cost the King £10,000 before he hath
made another as fit to serve him in the Navy as I am".

An amusing view of both Pepys the tactful official
and Pepys the honest diarist may be found on July 20,
1667. On that day the Clerk of the Acts writes to
Lord Belasyse about naval prizes at Hull. Here are
some of the beautifully phrased passages in his letter:

> My Lord, I have an interest in the Prize taken by
> Captain Hogg which by the report of the value of the
> Shipp may bee considerable to mee but without good
> caution against the imbezzlements I heare are likely to bee
> made I feare it may bee otherwise. But my Lord I esteeme
> it a part of my good fortune equall to all the rest that shee
> happens to be brought into a port where I have so noble a
> friend as your Lordshipp and in whose power it is to doe
> mee so much favour as by your Lordshipp's care all ready
> of providing for the security of the whole I am likely to
> finde the benefit of. . . . Soe that your Lordshipp will
> pardon mee if I adventure to begg the full advantage of your
> Lordshipp's kindness towards mee, which you have been
> pleased soe nobly to offer mee, and esteeming it my very
> great happiness to have fallen into your Lordshipp's pro-
> tection, at a time of my soe much needing it. . . .

On the same day we read in the Diary:

> Home to dinner and then to the office, we having
> dispatched away Mr. Oviatt to Hull, about our prizes
> there; and I have wrote a letter of thanks by him to Lord
> Bellasis who had writ to me to offer all his services for my
> interest there, but I dare not trust him.

Both during the Fire and the Plague Pepys stuck to
his post without any bragging, but with all the fears

and misgivings which these terrible events must have
provoked.

The famous entry in his Diary of September 2,
1666, in which he describes the outbreak of the Fire,
is not only the most remarkable entry in his Diary,
but as a narrative the most remarkable entry in any
diary. Most diarists fail conspicuously when they are
faced with events of great magnitude. They seem to
feel their inability to give an adequate account of them,
they strain their natural style in their endeavour to be
up to the mark or, as the French more aptly say, *à la
hauteur des circonstances*, and seldom, consequently,
does the result convey the deep impressions they
received. Pepys records his day hour by hour and
more fully than usual. Curiosity is succeeded by concern, concern by alarm, alarm by consternation,
consternation by panic. He never overloads the
recital of his observations, and the simplicity of his
personal impressions gradually unfolds the scene before
our eyes and makes us feel, as surely no other account
does, the full horror of it.

Let us follow him, though it must be rapidly,
through the day, the record of which transcribed
occupies five printed pages. Jane calls them up at
three in the morning. He goes to the window and
seeing a fire far off thinks little of it, and goes to bed
again. He has another look at seven, but still thinks
it nothing to bother about, and proceeds to tidy his
closet, "after yesterday cleaning". But Jane tells him
three hundred houses have been burned, so he goes off
to the Tower, taking a little boy with him, and there
sees "an infinite great fire" and is troubled for "poor
little Michell and our Sarah on the bridge". He

proceeds to the water-side, and sees the progress of the
fire and the tumult of the people running about to save
their goods. His all-observant eye catches a detail:
"The poor pigeons were loth to leave their houses, but
hovered about the windows and the balconys till they
were, some of them burned, their wings, and fell
down". He notices the fire catch a steeple "by which
pretty Mrs. —— lives, and whereof my old school
fellow Elborough is parson". He hastens to Whitehall,
sees the King and the Duke of York, and rushes off
with a message from them to the Lord Mayor. In
the City again he finds the Lord Mayor "like a man
spent". Pulling down houses is no good "as the fire
overtakes us faster than we can do it". It is now twelve
o'clock. He returns home, where he finds guests
whom he had invited, a Mr. Moone whom he had
asked "to look over my closet and please him with
the sight thereof", but there is too much excitement,
and they are interrupted by fresh news, although he
manages to have "an extraordinary good dinner", and
they were "as merry as at this time we could be". He
is soon off again to the City, observing the confusion
and the wind carrying the fire farther. He passes the
King and the Duke of York in their barge. Back again
to Whitehall, he meets his wife in St. James's Park.
He takes her on to the river, "so near the fire as we
could for smoke", and "almost burnt with the shower
of fire drops". After a visit to an alehouse night falls,
and then he gets the full view and describes the "most
horrid malicious bloody flame, not like the fine flame
of an ordinary fire", "we saw the fire as only an entire
arch of fire from this to the other side of the bridge
. . . it made me weep to see it"; "so home with a sad

heart", and he invites a friend in trouble, a Mr. Hater,
to stay with him.   But every moment fresh news
comes of the alarming growth of the fire, till at last he
and his household begin carrying his goods and his
papers and his bags of gold into the garden.   He ends
by saying that his guest got little rest because of the
noise in the house.

Yet we know that after all the activities and terrible
impressions of the day, in the midst of all this indescrib-
able confusion, with Mr. Hater tossing on his bed,
and Mrs. Pepys and Jane still dragging things into the
garden and London burning, he sat down and in rapid
shorthand recounted his experiences at a length which
cannot have occupied him much less than an hour.
Next morning he is up at four, the day is full of excitement, but the entry is much briefer.   With his diarist's
genius he knew the particular value of a first impression.

Anyone else writing about the Fire that day would
have dramatised his story, omitted all reference to
petty irrelevant events, would have worked up the
excitement, thinking it proper to subordinate and if
possible eliminate his own personality, and would have
been so overmastered by the magnitude of the cata-
strophe at the closing hour of the day, and indeed for
several days afterwards, as to have been quite incapable
of recalling his mood when that day dawned.   We do
not say that this might not be very effectively done.
Evelyn's account written the next day, although fine
in its way, is objective and impersonal, but we, as we
read it in the twentieth century, find ourselves looking
back to, not living on, September 2, 1666.   We do not
pass, as we do with Pepys, through each hour of the
day smelling the smoke, singed by the sparks, and

actually hoping in a moment of cheerfulness at dinner-time that it is not going to be so bad after all, till at last at night we struggle in panic to drag the furniture out of the house into the garden. If diary writing is not literature, let us be told in what great work of history or fiction an outstanding event has been better presented by a pen.

There is no detachable entry with regard to the Plague. The scourge weaves itself gradually through his days. It was not like the Fire, suddenly catastrophic, but our realisation of it is cumulative from the constant references. He never deserts his post, and does not indulge either in heroics or in morbid reflections. He just remarks to Coventry, "You took your turn of the sword, I must not grudge to take mine of the pesti-lence". He records its ravages with sorrow:

But, Lord! what a sad time it is to see no boats upon the River; and grass grows all up and down Whitehall court and nobody but poor wretches in the streets!

And his accustomed cheerfulness deserts him when he apprehends the danger he is running, "in case it should please God to call me away".

But quite an eloquent passage in a letter which he wrote to Lady Carteret on September 4 shows, although quite incidentally, his remarkable endurance:

I having stayed in the City till above 7400 died in one week and of these above 6000 of the Plague and little noise heard day and night but tolling of bells; till I could walk Lumber Street and not meet twenty persons from one end to the other, and not 50 upon the Exchange; till whole families 10 and 12 together have been swept away; till my very physician, Dr. Barnet who undertook to secure me against any infection, having survived the month of his own house being shut up, died himself of the Plague;

till the nights, though much lengthened are grown too short
to conceal the burials of those that died the day before,
people being thereby constrained to borrow daylight for
that service; lastly till I could find neither meat nor drink
safe, the butcheries being every where visited, my brewer's
house shut up and my baker, with his whole family, dead
of the Plague.

Some may inquire why Pepys with his love of detail
does not give us fuller particulars of his work at the
office. It was not because it was dull. On the contrary,
he was greatly absorbed in it. It was not because he
thought it might bore other people, because clearly he
had no other people in his mind's eye as he wrote.
Many diarists who have kept pretty full records
mention little or nothing about their professional
occupation. There may even be some difficulty in the
case of unknown people of ascertaining through the
medium of their diary what their profession was. This
seems to be quite natural, more especially when a man
finds enjoyment in writing his diary as Pepys did. The
monotony of his official or business routine prevents
that part of the day standing up in relief when he casts
back his glance over the hours spent as he sits down to
write.

As a matter of fact, when anything special is going
on at the Navy Office Pepys puts it down, and we are
given lively accounts of some of the quarrels and controversies. On most days he notes how long he spent
there. But in his full life there were so many more
coloured events which naturally had greater command
over his attention. Had he devoted half a page a day
to his official work, it would have been, considering
the rest of his day, abnormal and unlike Pepys. A

I

really busy long day at the office meant a short entry. Here is one; but no one can say it is bald.

May 6, 1665. Up, and all day at the office, but a little at dinner, and there late till past 12. So home to bed. pleased as I always am after I have rid a great deal of work, it being very satisfactory to me.

It has been said that the worst enemy to the reputation of the official Pepys is the Pepys of the Diary. But it must also be admitted that it is the Diary which has been the cause of all the voluminous research which has been made into the career of the official. Without the Diary his name would still be quite unknown, and none of his excellent work at the Admiralty would have been exhibited for our admiration.

CHAPTER VII

MUSIC, ART, AND LETTERS

THE Diary serves on the whole to enhance Pepys's official reputation, and justifies those of his contemporaries who rated him high as a Civil Servant of ability, loyal, courageous, and zealous in the discharge of his public duties. So much for the Clerk of the Acts and Secretary to the Navy. But the same can hardly be said of the President of the Royal Society, the art collector and musician.

In the realm of music, art, and letters, Pepys as an executant, composer, connoisseur, and author must be given quite a subordinate place. This need not in any way imply disparagement of him as a man of artistic tastes. The genuine appreciator may be almost as great an artist as the creator, and at any rate he often covers a very much larger field, as the creator is usually confined to one sphere. Lord Leighton, a nineteenth-century President of the Royal Academy, it is true, was a musician, a linguist, a poet, an architect, a classical scholar—"and then he paints", as Benjamin Jowett said when all this was related to him. Lord Leighton did not reach the first-rate in any of these spheres, but no one would dispute that he was an artist in the larger sense of the word.

Pepys, though not very highly educated (he had some difficulty in mastering the multiplication table), had the keenest appreciation of the refinements of the creative arts in many directions, and it is not only his appreciations, but his enthusiastic expression of them which pleases us so much. He may not have reached the third-rate even in any of the lines in which he dabbled, but then all the time he was being first-rate in another capacity, and of this he was entirely unconscious. He had a wonderfully keen sense of beauty both in art and in nature, derived not from culture but from instinctive good taste. It may be claimed that he had the artistic temperament which occasionally ran riot where female beauty was concerned.

Music came first and foremost. "Musique is the thing of the world that I love most", he says, and in a letter in later years he writes that "music is still my utmost luxury". The expressions of his joy in it must delight a musician's heart far more than his works would have done had he been a more proficient composer than he was. His appreciation of music, which was heightened by his practice of it, illustrates as well as anything the high level of aesthetic perception with which he was endowed.

His song "Beauty Retire" certainly and deservedly had some success. Knipp, who sang it "bravely", helped to popularise it, and Pepys says he finds it is "mightily cried up which I am not a little proud of". His own estimate of it was perhaps rather out of proportion to its merits, and two or three other songs he wrote were of no particular account. For "It is decreed" he employs Mr. Hingston the organist to set a bass, so we can gather from this that it was the air not the harmony

or accompaniment for which Pepys was responsible.
He learned to play the viol, the lute, the flute, the
flageolet, and the theorbo, and he sang—sang indeed
quite an appreciable part of his way through life. He
often sang in the morning in his room; as he walked
along the street we catch him "humming to myself
(which now a days is my constant practice since I began
to learn to sing) the trillo and find by use that it do come
upon me"; with a strange fellow-passenger in a boat he
sings as they are rowed down the river; while his wife
is shopping he stays in the coach with Mercer, "and
in a quarter of an hour I taught her the whole Larke's
song perfectly so excellent a ear hath she"; he sings
upon the leads of his house in the moonlight, in Hales's
studio while his wife is having her portrait painted,
and there were many evenings when singing or some
form of music was the chief entertainment, such, for
instance, as the Sunday on which he and his boy Tom
Edwards (who came from the King's Chapel) sang
psalms, "and then came in Mr. Hill and he sung with
us awhile; and he being gone, the boy and I again to
the singing of Mr. Porter's mottets"; and one moonlight night with his wife and Mercer he sang in the
garden for an hour, "with mighty pleasure to ourselves
and neighbours, by their casements opening".

Mrs. Pepys also has lessons in singing, but "poor
wretch her ear is so bad that it made me angry till the
poor wretch cried to see me so vexed at her". Samuel
had a high standard in this his favourite diversion.
Music indeed seems at one time to have distracted him
from his work. He confesses in fact that he is "fearful
of being too much taken with musique for fear of
returning to my old dotage thereon and so neglect my

business as I used to do". We can hardly condemn Pepys as a mundane materialist when we see the effect music has on him. He writes after seeing the *Virgin Martyr*:

To the King's House to see "the virgin Martyr" . . . that which did please me beyond anything in the whole world was the wind-musique when the angel comes down, which is so sweet that it ravished me and indeed in a word did wrap up my soul so that it made me really sick, just as I have formerly been when in love with my wife; that neither then nor all the evening going home and at home, I was able to think of anything but remained all night transported so as I could not believe that ever any music hath that real command over the soul of a man as this did upon me; and makes me resolve to practice wind-musique and to make my wife do the like.

His taste in music was simple; anything difficult, elaborate, or even foreign puzzled him.

. . . here I did hear Mrs Manuel and one of the Italians her gallant sing well. But yet I confess I am not delighted so much with it as to admire it; for, not understanding the words, I lose the benefit of the vocalitys of the musick and it proves only instrumental; and therefore was more pleased to hear Knepp sing two or three little English things that I understood, though the composition of the other, and performance, was very fine.

Pepys went so far as to conceive a scheme of music or "a better theory of musique", and makes resolutions to develop this "theory of musique not yet ever made in the world". He goes so far as to write out fair some of his "musique notions", and refers to it as "getting the scale of musique without book, which I have done to perfection backward and forward". But that was as far as it got.

In a letter to Dr. Charlett in 1700 he defines in rather more pompous language the importance of music. He begins:

Musick; a science peculiarly productive of a pleasure that no state of life, publick or private, secular or sacred; no difference of age or season; no temper of mind or condition of health exempt from present anguish; nor, lastly, distinction of quality, renders either improper, untimely, or unentertaining. Witness the universal gusto we see it followed with, wherever to be found, by all where leisure and purse can bear it.

But in the next sentence, which contains no less than 160 words, in his desire to be impressive to the Reverend Doctor he becomes incomprehensible.

So far as painting is concerned there is little to be said. Pepys was chiefly interested in portrait painting, portraits of himself; and in this, likeness was the one element he looked for. He is pleased with Hales's picture, because he thinks it is "mighty like", and the sheet of music he is holding (his song "Beauty Retire") is also approved, "being painted very true". Hales on one occasion accompanies him to the Whitehall picture gallery; he is not much impressed, and thinks Hales's pictures by comparison to be very good. In 1669 he had four panels of his dining-room painted by Henry Dankers the landscape painter. But he absolutely insisted on the "Landskipp" in his own portrait by Hales being "put out". In his Naval Minutes he deplores that we have no seascape painters like the Dutch.

The collections in his library include good drawings, and he invested in "many excellent prints" by Robert Nanteuil the French engraver. But prints for the most part were not included in his collections because of their artistic merit, but because they fitted into the particular series to which they respectively belong. In art and objects of virtu the curious appealed to him more than the beautiful.

To Pepys as an author only a passing attention need be paid. The one work we have from Pepys's pen is his Memoir of the Royal Navy, or, to give it its full title, *Memoires relating to the State of the Royal Navy of England for ten years Determin'd December 1688*. There is a note which explains that the Memoirs were published in order to defend the special Commission of 1686 against attacks raised to discredit them. Pepys had been driven from office in 1679; the office of Lord High Admiral had been placed in commission, with the result that for five years the higher administration of the Navy was in the hands of incompetent and inexperienced men; the effective force at sea was reduced, the ships in harbour allowed to fall out of repair, and waste and neglect appeared in every department. In 1686 Pepys was recalled to his office and a special Commission appointed. The Memoirs were written to show up the period of mismanagement and to defend the special Commission.

The book, which, apart from the tables appended to it, can be read in an hour or so, is little more than a controversial pamphlet. As an official with the facts at his finger-ends he was able to make out his case in a clear, business-like way without any exaggerated polemics or recriminations. The book ends with a general reflection on the Navy in his religious vein:

And yet not such that (even at its Zenith) it both did and suffer'd sufficient to teach us that there is something above both That and Us that governs the world. To which (Incomprehensible) alone be Glory.

He refers to this book as "the contents of one chapter of a greater number wherewith the world may some time or other be more largely entertained upon the general subject of the *Navalia* of England". It certainly would make a very small chapter in such a work, and while it may be said to deal effectively with the particular points of dispute which were in question at that moment, there is nothing in it to make us suppose that the author was capable of writing the larger work. On the contrary, we should judge from the style and rather clumsy diction, from the bald recital of facts which were easily accessible to him, from the trite summaries of the qualities necessary to a good administration and the absence of any generalisations based on historical knowledge, that the writing of a full history was quite beyond his reach. As it was not want of time, opportunity, or access to material which hindered him in the greater task, it would not be an extravagant speculation to conclude that it was this little effort of his which revealed to him his inability to tackle the larger book. The two works we have from Pepys's pen, the Diary and the Memoirs, are at poles very far apart. But neither our wonder at the Diary nor our admiration for the diligent official should make us pretend that this effort of his in historical controversy is a work of any consequence at all. Had it not been for the Diary this little book would have remained in oblivion, or at most received passing mention from a naval historian. The only contemporary mention of it to be found apart from Evelyn's, which has already been quoted, comes from a Frenchman, F. Misson, who says:

Pour être bien informé de tout ce qui regard la Marine Royale d'Angleterre, il faut lire le livre qu'en a écrit, il n'y a pas long-temps, M. Samuel Pepys Secrétaire de l'Amirauté etc.[1]

Pepys once wrote a romance when he was an undergraduate, and of this he gives us his opinion when he was thirty.

1663/64, January 30. This evening being in a humour of making all things even and clear in the world, I tore some old papers; among others, a romance which (under the title of " Love a Cheate ") I began ten years ago at Cambridge; and at this time reading it over to-night I liked it very well, and wondered a little at myself at my vein at that time when I wrote it, doubting that I cannot do so well now if I would try.

It has been suggested that Pepys was lacking in imagination. This is probably true. We do not come to this conclusion so much from his inability to write a book as from the style and method of his Diary. Imagination is no help to the recollection and recital of events; on the contrary, it may be a hindrance, and it can even be an obstacle to complete honesty.

His literary tastes, his criticisms and his preferences in books we find thickly scattered through the Diary. Some of them are fitting to the official, some natural to the collector, some unexpectedly disclosing the scholar as when casually he quotes Epictetus, some characteristic of the "curious" man, and a few indicative of the undisciplined moods of the sensualist. We can trace appreciation of beauty, of humour, of the strange, the abnormal, and the antique, and of the purely

---

[1] *Mémoires et observations faites par un voyageur en Angleterre,* F. Misson, 1698.

bawdy, but no penetrating or subtle understanding of the higher realms of literature. His was a mundane, orderly, shrewd intelligence, not an imaginative, romantic, or finely discriminating mind. Literary taste cannot be judged by the contents of a collector's library. But we have many of his opinions to guide us.

Milton in Restoration society was of course not popular. It was therefore only in accordance with the fashion that he did not put Milton's works in his library. But after the Revolution he repairs this omission. Chaucer, he admits, is "without doubt a very fine poet" and he reads him "with great pleasure". Of Erasmus's *De scribendis epistolis* he writes:

A very good book especially one letter of advice to a courtier most true and good which made me once resolve to tear out the two leaves it was writ in but I forbore it.

Butler's *Hudibras* gave him a deal of trouble. He was anxious to be in line with popular opinion but too honest in his Diary to say he liked it when he did not. He buys it at once for 2s. 6d.

But when I come to read it, it is so silly an abuse of the Presbeter Knight going to the warrs that I am ashamed of it,

so he sells it for eighteen pence. But finding it "so cried up to be the example of wit" he buys it again and reads it again.

It hath not a good liking in me though I had tried but twice or three times reading to bring myself to think it witty.

Apparently he eventually became a convert to it, for we find him years later taking it with him and reading it on the Tangier expedition.

Pepys's correspondence has already been referred to. There are no letters of his which call for special comment as literary productions; nor are there any passages in letters received by him which testify to his having held on account of his talents a conspicuous position in the world of art and letters.

As to foreign languages, Pepys could read French and also Spanish and purchased many books in those languages. He also says that he understood a friar who preached in the Queen's Chapel in Portuguese. In the curious jumble of languages he employed when he wrote certain passages most of which are omitted from the printed edition of the Diary he used Spanish words more often than French. There are several mentions in the Diary of the purchase and also the reading of Spanish books, sometimes in translation, but a sentence in the entry of April 28, 1669, seems to show he could read them in the original. "This morning Mr. Sheres sent me in two volumes, Mariana his *History of Spaine*, in Spanish an excellent book, and I am much obliged to him for it."

Shakespeare was not one of Pepys's favourites, but as an ardent playgoer he witnesses the performance of many of the plays several times. Shakespeare, we must remember, had not in the late seventeenth century the hall-marked reputation and pre-eminent position which is accorded him to-day. Moreover, all sorts of liberties were taken with the plays. There was a semi-operatic version of *Hamlet* produced by Davenant, songs and dances were introduced into *The Tempest*, and there was an alternative version of *Romeo and Juliet*.

He records in his Diary nine occasions on which he

saw *Hamlet.* Betterton's acting of the Prince of Denmark he declares to be "beyond imagination" and when someone else takes the part he regrets it. He thinks it "a most excellent play in all respects but especially in divertisement, though it be a deep tragedy". On one of the occasions his attention is completely distracted by the King's disturbing passages with Lady Castlemaine.

The Tempest he saw several times; "the most innocent play as ever I saw. The play has no great wit but yet good above ordinary plays." He thinks it "full of good variety", he learns "the tune of the seamans' dance", and the Echo song pleases him mightily.

One night he breaks his resolution not to go so often to the play and he turns in to see *Twelfth Night.* But he takes no pleasure in it and considers it "a silly play and not related at all to the name or day", and when he sees it again later he declares it to be "one of the weakest plays that ever I saw on the stage".

On *Henry V.* he makes no comment, nor on *Othello* except that a very pretty lady who sat by him "called out" when Desdemona was smothered. *The Merry Wives* "did not please me at all in no part". One visit to the *Midsummer Night's Dream* was enough for him. It was a play "which I have never seen before nor shall ever again for it is the most insipid ridiculous play that ever I saw in my life". A first night of *Romeo and Juliet* produces the comment: "It is a play of itself the worst that ever I heard in my life and the worst acted that ever I saw these people do". *The Taming of the Shrew* he condemns as "a silly play".

Pepys's comments on Shakespeare remind one of

George III.'s. "Was there ever", said His Majesty to
Fanny Burney, "such stuff as great part of Shakespeare? only one must not say so. . . . Is there not
sad stuff? What? what?. . . . I know it is not to be
said. But it's true. Only it's Shakespeare and nobody
dare abuse him"; or of Cobbett who writes with
sarcasm of "the practice to extol every line of Shakespeare to the skies; not to admire Shakespeare has been
deemed to be a proof of want of understanding and
taste".

Beaumont and Fletcher did not always find favour
with Pepys either. He sees *The Knight of the Burning
Pestle*, "which pleased me not at all". *The Spanish
Curate*, however, he thought "pretty good". *Cupid's
Revenge* had some good in it, but he did not like "the
whole body of it". *The Humorous Lieutenant* "has
little good in it", and *The Storm*, by Fletcher, is "but
so so methinks". Over *Philaster* he has one of those
affectionate remembrances of his boyhood: "It is
pretty to see how I could remember almost all along
ever since I was a boy, Arethusa, the part which I was
to have acted at Sir Robert Cooke's; and it was very
pleasant to me, but more to think what a ridiculous
thing it would have been for me to have acted a beautiful woman". In another of Beaumont and Fletcher's
plays, *The Sea Voyage*, he greatly admires Knipp in
"her part of sorrow". He goes to her house afterwards,
and while waiting for her "je did kiss her ancilla, which
is so mighty belle". But we must not follow him after
the play, otherwise we shall come across those little
dots which occur even in the largest edition of the
Diary. Nevertheless we must just go round behind the
footlights with him once.

To the King's house; and there going in met with Knipp and she took us up into the tireing rooms; and to the womens' shift where Nell was dressing herself and was all unready, and is very pretty, prettier than I thought. And into the scene room and there sat down and she gave us fruit. . . . But Lord, to see how they were both painted would make a man mad and did make me loath them; and what base company of men comes among them and how lewdly they talk! And how poor the men are in clothes and yet what a show they make on the stage by candle light is very observable. But to see how Nell cursed for having so few people in the pit was pretty; the other house carrying away all the people at the new play and is said nowadays to have generally most company as being better players. By and by into the pit and there saw the play which is pretty good.

Pepys indeed was rather a captious critic; this can be seen with regard to sermons as well as plays. He was not to be allured by the reputation of the author nor by plays which were "mightily cried up". Dryden's play *The Wilde Gallant* he calls "so poor a thing as I never saw in my life almost". On the other hand, he describes *The Siege of Rhodes* as "the best poem that ever was wrote". But there were many plays of which he approved, such as *The Witts*, "which I like exceedingly"; Davenant's *Love and Honour*, "a very good plot"; *The Mad Couple*, "a pretty pleasant play", or *The Committee*, which has "a great deal of good invention in it". A play called *Sir Martin Mar-all* gets an unexpected amount of praise: "Am mightily pleased with it and think it mighty witty and the fullest of proper matter for mirth that ever was writ". He was nervous as to how *The Duke of Lerma*, by Howard, would be received, as it was "designed to reproach the King with his mistresses", but he commends it as "a very good and most serious play". He reads *The Adventures of Five Hours*, by Samuel Tuke, and thinks it "a most excellent play".

Pepys was a devoted patron of the theatre. He attached almost more importance to the acting than to the play itself. The social atmosphere of the theatre also appealed to him. He met there friends and acquaintances, and watched with amusement the presence of royalty or notables whose goings on were duly noted by him.

Here [at the Royal Theatre] I saw my Lord Falconbridge and his Lady, my Lady Mary Cromwell who looks as well as I have known her and well clad; but when the House began to fill she put on her vizard and so kept it on all the play; which of late is become a great fashion among the ladies which hides their whole face.

He generally sat in the pit (the stalls), and bought his refreshments at the King's playhouse from Orange Moll, who also acted as a messenger between him and the actors when he wanted to go "behind". His devotion to this form of entertainment was very strong. "Sat by Colonel Reames who understands and loves a play as well as I do and I love him for it." But finding it interferes with his work, he classes playgoing with drink and makes a resolution to abstain. He is only successful for a while. We find the conscientious official getting the upper hand when he writes after refusing an invitation to go to the play:

I hope I shall ever do so and above all things it is considerable that my mind was never in my life in so good condition of quiet as it has been since I have followed my business and seen myself to get greater and greater fitness in my employment and honour every day more than another.

However he succumbs, and the number of times he went to one or other of the playhouses in the Diary years can almost be counted in hundreds. Pepys was no highbrow, but his value as a critic rests on his absolute independence of mind and his refusal to be biassed either by popular opinion or by any accepted intellectual standards. He had a long experience, but always retained an individual opinion.

If costume can be regarded as a form of art, here again we find Pepys a critic, a judge, and a keen devotee. The references to clothes throughout the Diary are innumerable. With regard to himself he wanted to dress up to the standard which he considered was due to his position, and, as already shown, he erred on the side of ostentation. He took great delight in the choice and purchase of clothes.

My tailor brings me home my fine new coloured cloth suit my cloak lined with plush—as good a suit as ever I wore in my life and mighty neat to my great content.

Of his wife's clothes he was more often than not very critical.

Anon comes down my wife dressed in her second mourning with her black moyre waistcoat and short petti-coat laced with silver lace so basely that I could not endure to see her . . . so that I was horrid angry and would not go to our intended meeting which vexed me to the blood.

But there were also occasions when he approved and found her "fine and handsome".

Whether it was a song or a dance, a picture, a book, an opera or a play, a coat or a petticoat, Pepys had a decided opinion on it; it might be appreciation, criticism, or condemnation. He cultivated the art of acute

K

observation. As to whether he expressed his views as tersely and effectively in words as he did in writing we can never know; but we should think it very improbable. At any rate he shows us in his record that there was one vice of which he was absolutely free, and that was indifference.

CHAPTER VIII

PEPYS AT HOME

ALTHOUGH a large field is covered by Pepys's observations on the Navy, on the Court, on politics, on pictures, books, and plays, it is the domestic part of the Diary which has chiefly contributed to give it fame as a unique human document. From "up betimes" until "so to bed", not only are we made to feel his personality, but we are introduced to a domestic interior which has the sharpness of detail of a Dutch picture.

It has already been noted that the first entries of the Diary as we now have them are unlikely to have been Pepys's first attempts at diary writing. However that may be, we find him at once adopting the method which he maintained to the end. Many diarists begin by brief notes of engagements, accounts and lists of people seen, and then gradually expand as the diary habit grips them. A considerable number, if not the majority, ignore domestic details altogether. Pepys seems to have made up his mind from the outset that he was going to write down everything he could remember, both public and private.

The first entry is not a long one. It was written on a Sunday. He tells us what he wore, the text of the sermon he heard, what he had for dinner, how his wife

burned her hand dressing the turkey, what he did in
the afternoon, what he observed in the streets, and
where and with whom he supped. On Monday he
does more so he tells us more. From the arrival of a
dozen bottles of sack in the early morning to the
eating of a slice of brawn before he goes to bed, every
episode in the day is related. So we see at once that
we are going to be told everything, and no day
passes without our having a personal and domestic
setting for the day's doings, a setting, too, which is not
coldly objective but which is coloured by his own
varying mood.

To detach quotations throughout the Diary in
order to reproduce the detailed picture is manifestly
impossible. Sequence is indispensable for a full
appreciation of Pepys's method. Failing that, we may
follow an episode which perhaps may be considered a
minor episode in the ups and downs in Samuel's
household covering the space of about a month. But
it must always be remembered that the extracts suffer
from being detached from their context where they
are bedded in the full account of the day's doings, when
he is doing his work, talking with officials, listening to
sermons, going to the play, buying books, gathering
Court gossip, examining tar, conning his measuring
ruler, and boxing his boy's ears.

The dramatis personae of the episode are Pembleton,
the dancing master, and Mary Ashwell, a sort of companion to Mrs. Pepys. All went well at first. Pembleton teaches both Pepys and his wife. They dance
after supper, "late and merry at it and so weary
to bed". This was on May 6, 1663. On May 15 the
trouble begins.

May 15th. . . . home, where I found it almost night, and my wife and the dancing-master alone above, not dancing but talking. Now so deadly full of jealousy I am that my heart and head did so cast about and fret that I could not do any business possibly, but went out to my office, and anon late home again and ready to chide at every thing, and then suddenly to bed and could hardly sleep, yet durst not say any thing, but was forced to say that I had bad news from the Duke concerning Tom Hater as an excuse to my wife, who by my folly has too much opportunity given her with the man, who is a pretty neat black man, but married. But it is a deadly folly and plague that I bring upon myself to be so jealous and by giving myself such an occasion more than my wife desired of giving her another month's dancing. Which however shall be ended as soon as I can possibly.

May 17th. . . . then to talk with my wife till after supper, and so to bed having another small falling out and myself vexed with my old fit of jealousy about her dancing-master. But I am a fool for doing it.

May 19th. . . . then by water, (taking Pembleton with us) over the water to the Half-way House, where we played at nine-pins, and there my damned jealousy took fire, he and my wife being of a side and I seeing of him take her by the hand in play, though I now believe he did [it] only in passing and sport.

May 21st. . . . Pembleton being there again, we fell to dance a country dance or two, and so to supper and bed. But being at supper my wife did say something that caused me to oppose her in, she used the word devil, which vexed me, and among other things I said I would not have her to use that word, upon which she took me up most scornfully, which, before Ashwell and the rest of the world, I know not now-a-days how to check, as I would heretofore, for less than that would have made me strike her.

May 26th. . . . By and by my mind being in great trouble I went home to see how things were, and there I found as I doubted Mr. Pembleton with my wife, and nobody else in the house, which made me almost mad. . . . I continued in my chamber vexed and angry till he went away, pretending aloud, that I might hear, that he could not stay, and Mrs. Ashwell not being within they could not dance. And, Lord! to see how my jealousy wrought so far that I went softly up to see whether any of the beds were out of order or no, which I found not, but that did not content me, but I staid all the evening walking, and though anon my wife came up to me and would have spoke of business to me, yet I construed it to be but impudence, and though my heart full yet I did say nothing, being in a great doubt what to do.

May 27th. . . . so home, where I find my wife in a musty humour, and tells me before Ashwell that Pembleton had been there, and she would not have him come in unless I was there, which I was ashamed of; but, however, I had rather it should be so than the other way. So to my office, to put things in order there, and by and by comes Pembleton, and word is brought me from my wife thereof that I might come home. So I sent word that I would have her go dance, and I would come presently. So being at a great loss whether I should appear to Pembleton or no, and what would most proclaim my jealousy to him, I at last resolved to go home.

May 31st. Lay long in bed talking with my wife, and do plainly see that her distaste (which is beginning now in her again) against Ashwell arises from her jealousy of me and her, and my neglect of herself, which indeed is true, and I to blame; but for the time to come I will take care to remedy all. So up and to church, where I think I did see Pembleton, whatever the reason is I did not perceive him to look up towards my wife, nor she much towards him; however I could hardly keep myself from being troubled that he was there, which is a madness not to be excused now that his coming to my house is past, and I hope all likelyhood of her having occasion to converse with him again.

June 2nd. My wife did also this evening tell me a story of Ashwell stealing some new ribbon from her, a yard or

two, which I am sorry to hear, and I fear my wife do take
a displeasure against her, that they will hardly stay together,
which I should be sorry for, because I know not where
to pick such another out anywhere . . . then home, and,
God forgive me, did from my wife's unwillingness to tell
me whither she had sent the boy, presently suspect that he
was gone to Pembleton's, and from that occasion grew so
discontented that I could hardly speak or sleep all night. . . .

June 4th. . . . yet I could not get off my suspicions, she
having a mind to go into Fenchurch Street before she went
out for good and all with me, which I must needs construe
to be to meet Pembleton, when she afterwards told me it
was to buy a fan that she had not a mind that I should know
of, and I believe it is so. Specially I did by a wile get out
of my boy that he did not yesterday go to Pembleton's or
thereabouts but only was sent all that time for some starch,
and I did see him bringing him some, and yet all this
cannot make my mind quiet . . . my mind in trouble for
my wife, being jealous of her spending the day, though
God knows I have no great reason. Yet my mind is
troubled.

June 5th. . . . a little troubled to see my wife take no
more pleasure with Ashwell, but neglect her and leave
her at home.

June 6th. . . . so home to supper and bed. My mind being
troubled to think into what a temper of neglect I have
myself flung my wife into by my letting her learn to dance,
that it will require time to cure her of, and I fear her going
into the country will but make her worse.

June 7th. . . . my wife and I had an angry word or two
upon discourse of our boy. . . . It troubles me to see that
every small thing is enough now-a-days to bring a difference
between us.

June 8th. After dinner my wife and I had a little
jangling, in which she did give me the lie, which vexed me,
so that finding my talking did but make her worse, and
that her spirit is lately come to be other than it used to be,

and now depends upon her having Ashwell by her, before whom she thinks I shall not say nor do anything of force to her, which vexes me and makes me wish that I had better considered all that I have of late done concerning my bringing my wife to this condition of heat, I went up vexed to my chamber and there fell examining my new concordance.

June 9th. Presently after my coming home comes Pembleton, whether by appointment or no I know not, or whether by a former promise that he would come once before my wife's going into the country, but I took no notice of, let them go up and Ashwell with them to dance, which they did, and I staid below in my chamber, but Lord! how I listened and laid my ear to the door, and how I was troubled when I heard them stand still and not dance. Anon they made an end and had done, and so I suffered him to go away, and spoke not to him, though troubled in my mind, but showed no discontent to my wife, believing that this is the last time I shall be troubled with him.

June 11th. . . . spent the evening with my wife, and she and I did jangle mightily about her cushions that she wrought with worsteds the last year, which are too little for any use, but were good friends by and by again. But one thing I must confess I do observe, which I did not before, which is, that I cannot blame my wife to be now in a worse humour than she used to be, for I am taken up in my talk with Ashwell, who is a very witty girl, that I am not so fond of her as I used and ought to be, which now I do perceive I will remedy, but I would to the Lord I had never taken any, though I cannot have a better than her.

June 14th. I do see great cause every day to curse the time that ever I did give way to the taking of a woman for her, though I could never have had a better, and also the letting of her learn to dance, by both which her mind is so devilishly taken off her business and minding her occasions, and besides has got such an opinion in her of my being jealous, that it is never to be removed, I fear, nor hardly my trouble that attends it; but I must have patience.

June 15th. Thence home, but finding my wife gone,
I took coach and after her to her inn, where I am troubled
to see her forced to sit in the back of the coach, though
pleased to see her company none but women and one
parson; she I find is troubled at all, and I seemed to make
a promise to get a horse and ride after them; and so,
kissing her often, and Ashwell once, I bid them adieu. . . .
I up to my wife's closett, and there played on my viallin
a good while, and without supper anon to bed, sad for
want of my wife, whom I love with all my heart, though of
late she has given me some troubled thoughts.

The cruder episodes, such, for instance, as the night
on which his wife attacked him with red-hot tongs, one
can well imagine him recording. But here is a confession of petty jealousy made by its victim—groundless suspicions confessed to be groundless yet continu-
ing to be suspicions. Surely no human being has ever
been able to convey so subtly through his own un-
reasonable weakness his own transparent sincerity,
and to display such astonishing candour without
seeming to make a confession. The self-analyst
cudgelling his brains in his attempt to dissect his
actions and motives would never be able to give such
a picture of human misgiving and petty irrationality.
Passages such as these seem to prove that Pepys to a
degree which no diarist has ever reached was able to
dismiss completely from his mind as he wrote any idea
whatever even of the most imaginary reader's eye.

To food there are references innumerable. On
occasions the quantity reaches the proportions described by Parson Woodforde when he dined with
the Squire. But Pepys regarded his own dinners very
much as a gauge of his social status, and was mightily
pleased when he could afford a dinner which showed

him to be a man of substance. This curious, perhaps
it may be called rather pleasant, form of ostentation is
very common, more especially with social climbers.
Lavish expenditure on food is a testimony to their
consequence. But while Pepys behaved himself no
doubt with great dignity at the dinner-table, allowing
people to suppose that such fare was habitual to him
and nothing out of the ordinary, he tells us in the
Diary the efforts of preparations which went on behind
the scenes. Trollope gives an excellent description in
Miss Mackenzie of a pretentious dinner where the
effort failed because there was not enough to go round.
Pepys took such pains that he seldom had a failure, at
any rate in quantity, except the unfortunate day when
Coventry came in unexpectedly and the mutton was
underdone. One dinner may be described.

On January 12 (1662/63) he calls in after his work
is done to see Lady Batten, his object being to get
some oranges from her "for my feast to-morrow".
He succeeds, takes them home, and finds Mrs. Pepys
occupied with her new gown with which she is mightily
pleased. But Samuel is angry that more preparation
has not been made "against to-morrow's feast", gets
into a passion and goes discontented to bed. Elizabeth
Pepys is up at five the next morning buying provisions
at the market. There is a moment of doubt as to
whether the jack will carry the chine of beef, but all
goes well, the cook comes, Pepys hurries off to his
office, and we can hardly expect that he did a good day's
work there. He returns home and the company arrive:
"Dr. Clarke and his lady, his sister and a she-cozen
and Mr. Pierce and his wife ".

The eight of them sit down.

. . . after oysters, at first course, a hash of rabbits, a lamb and a rare chine of beef. Next a great dish of roasted fowl, cost me about 30s and a tart and then fruit and cheese. My dinner was noble and enough. I had my house mighty clean and neat; my room below with a good fire in it; my dining room above, and my chamber being made a withdrawing room; and my wife's a good fire also. I find my new table very proper, and will hold nine or ten people well but eight with great room.

Cards came after dinner, and for supper there was "a good sack posset and cold meat". The guests left at ten o'clock; "their company was very fine". Mrs. Clarke was the success of the evening, "a very witty, fine lady, though a little conceited and proud". He does not on this occasion specially mention Mrs. Pierce, who was "la belle Pierce" whose "beautiful company" Pepys enjoyed rather too much. He expresses himself highly pleased with "our management of this day", goes to bed "weary", and has just a misgiving as he writes at the conclusion of the entry: "I believe this day's feast will cost me near £5".

All this may be trivial and even frivolous, but we are obliged to recognise that the method of his narrative gives the analytical psychologist a great store of information. Pepys was as critical of food as he was of everything else. After a dinner with Sir W. Hickes he writes:

He did give us the meanest dinner of beef shoulder and umbles of venison . . . and a few pigeons and all in the meanest manner that ever I did see to the basest degree.

Drink was a temptation, but his resolutions against excess appear to have been successful. Here is a bad day:

What at dinner and supper I drink I know not how, of my own accord, so much wine that I was even almost foxed and my head aked all night; so home and to bed without prayers, which I never did yet since I come to the house of a Sunday night; I being now so out of order that I durst not read prayers for fear of being perceived by my servants in what case I was.

There may be some doubt whether he was rigidly carrying out his resolution when at the Guildhall he drinks "hypocras". He excuses himself to himself by saying "it being to the best of my present judgment only a mixed compound drink and not any wine".

But Pepys was neither a glutton nor a drunkard; he was not a dissolute profligate nor a frivolous fool any more than he was a skilled musician or a learned scholar. In his nine years' revelation there is no emphasis laid on incidents which would justify us in condemning him or praising him in any of these directions. On the contrary, everything is presented in its exact relation to the rest. It is our faulty sense of proportion based on insincerity which makes us jump at wrong conclusions. We conceive that certain things ought not to be said or ought not to be noticed. When they are said and noticed by a man who says and notices everything we immediately endow them with exaggerated significance. Pepys is not to blame. It is our habitual lack of candour and preference for concealment which blinds us to the perfect balance of Pepys's narrative. To cull all references to food, drink, clothes, escapades, and domestic quarrels and string them together would of course ruin the picture. Each reference fits into its place as an indispensable link in the sequence of the day's events. In wrenching them from their context—and we cannot resist doing it sometimes—we give them an emphasis they do not really possess.

Undoubtedly, however, his habit of never forgetting to insert the domestic and personal details allows us an insight into a human being of which few other examples exist, if indeed any.

Of all the intimate circumstances of domestic life, the relationship between man and wife is naturally the most important. Whatever be the profession or occupation of a man his relations with his wife influence and colour the incidents of his daily life to a special degree. Instances could be quoted of bachelor diarists either leaving off writing when they marry or converting a diary of reflection and self-analysis into a perfunctory objective record. The wife takes the place of the diary as confidant. Wolfe Tone wrote his diary for his wife, and left off writing when he was with her. But most diarists are very reticent with regard to their wives, some confining themselves to occasional affectionate references. Others have expressed their devotion in special passages, such, for instance, as the first Lord Shaftesbury's entry on the death of his wife, which comes as a surprise in an otherwise brief objective record. Sir Henry Slingsby in the early seventeenth century and Egmont in the eighteenth century refer to their wives with affectionate appreciation, and the grumbling Lord Wariston inserts many passages showing his realisation of the influence exercised over him by the remarkable woman to whom he was married. Even Benjamin Haydon in the midst of all his invective and vituperation reserves nothing but words of the deepest affection for his Mary.

But if the relationship is strained or unfortunate,

the honest diarist will not fail to note it. Adam Eyre,
a Yorkshire country gentleman of the middle of the
seventeenth century, found his wife's temper a sore
trial and refers to it in many entries ("This morne
my wife began after her old manner to braule and
revile me . . ."). Sir Humphrey Mildmay, High
Sheriff of Essex, 1636, quarrels a good deal with his
wife, but is fair enough to admit that he himself is
sometimes to blame ("Worthily did I acknowledge
the error to be mine"). Thomas Turner, after several
altercations with his wife Peggy, puts his dilemma down
in black and white:

I think I have tried all experiments to make our life's
happy but they have all failed. The opposition seems to
be naturally in our tempers—not arising from spitefulness
but an opposition that seems indicated by our very make
and constitution.

But William Jones's candid record contained the fullest
account of these intimate domestic relations. We say
"contained", because in a fit of remorse he destroyed
the separate volume in which he had concentrated and
enlarged upon them and which he called "the book of
Domestic Lamentations". But in his main diary there
are a number of references to his wife, often satirical
("She not only plays cards and stirs a fire but does
everything else better than her dear husband"),
sometimes affectionate ("my old mate", "my old rib").
His varying mood is shown and his wife's characteristics graphically described. But, trying as Mrs. Jones
appears to have been, we can gather from his own
account that his constant presence in the house must
have been a high trial to her.

In fact all references to wives, however acrimonious

and unsettled the relationship may have been, seem
to have a fairness on the part of the diarist which arises
from the fact that there is no single summing up, but
day-to-day observation, in which self-blame inevitably
alternates with irritation and temper. Women on the
whole appear to be more reticent, although we have
instances in Anne Clifford and in Mary Rich, Countess
of Warwick, of very bitter references to the short-
comings of their partners. The tragedy of the grievance
against her husband nursed by Jane Welsh Carlyle
in the pages of her diary was never fully disclosed,
because she burned most of it. Sufficient, however,
remained to give Carlyle a terrible shock after she
died.

So we see that some husbands and wives are more
disposed to confide in their diaries than in one another.
But the method adopted by Pepys differs from that of
any other diarist.

A collection of the numerous references by Pepys
to his wife would give us an excellent portrait of her,
and also, in spite of its simplicity, a rather subtle analysis
of their relations together. Pepys is not only candid,
but exceedingly fair. He acknowledges his faults and
admits he gives her cause for complaint, and when she
flies at him he generally justifies her. His affection
for her is based on sentiment and gratitude, but she
casts no spell over him.

The altercations, bickering and reconciliations, the
praise and the blame are never detached and enlarged
on. Pepys would never have kept a book of Domestic
Lamentations. His optimistic nature made him soon
forget all that was unpleasant, and it was he on the
whole who always hastened the time for making up.

Elizabeth Pepys was half French. Her father, Alexander, Sieur de St. Michel, was a Huguenot who came over in the retinue of Henrietta Maria. He seems to have been a scatter-brained individual, and we note a certain inconsequence and obstinacy in Elizabeth which she may have inherited from her father. She married Pepys when she was 15, five years before the Diary begins, and she died in 1669, about five months after it concludes. There is some beauty in the picture of her as St. Katherine by Hales but very little in the bust by John Dwight of Fulham.

Pepys was very much in love with her to begin with, and a sense of gratitude to her for having stood by him and helped him in his years of poverty never left him. Their quarrels were due to both of them having quick tempers and both suffering from the pangs of jealousy, Mrs. Pepys with good cause, Samuel (as we have already seen) groundlessly. They quarrel over trivialities: over the dog, over cooking, over clothes, over jewels, over the accounts, and incessantly over servants. It always seems dangerously near permanent incompatibility, specially when twice he pulls her nose and gives her a bad blow on the eye. But in between the quarrels there are invariable notes of appreciation, praise, and affection, and the flare-up never lasts for more than a day or two.

On the whole, we are heartily sorry for Elizabeth Pepys: but we must remember that it is Pepys himself who shows us that we ought to be. After the false alarms over the prospect of the birth of a child she settles down and certainly tries her utmost to make herself into a fitting companion for her extraordinarily versatile husband. But her want of success is pathetic. Her letters are "so false spelt" that they make the punctilious official angry, and he is shocked at her method of keeping accounts; "when she do miss a sum she do add something to other things to make it". He teaches her arithmetic—which, by the way, was not one of his strong subjects—and he hopes by studying the globes that he will "bring her to understand many fine things". A master teaches her singing, but the enraptured lover of music finds she has no ear. The dancing lessons, as we have seen, only lead to trouble. She is taught drawing, but that does not seem to have come to anything. The only thing he praises is her playing of the flageolet. She is lonely and wants a companion, and in one of the scenes when she took to "blubbering" she threatens to go to France, "then all come out that I loved pleasure and denied her any". The most serious of the quarrels was caused by her jealousy of Deb Willet, whom she finds Pepys kissing. It was by no means his worst offence towards her, but she saw it with her own eyes. She not only rages and calls Samuel "a false rotten hearted rogue", but ingeniously thinks out a method of touching him on the raw by telling him she is a Roman Catholic, which of course "troubled" him.

Pepys shows up in this episode in the worst possible light. The entry in which he actually begins by saying that his heart was "full of joy" because he thought he had succeeded in the monstrous deception on his wife is perhaps the most discreditable in all their relations. Yet it is in that very entry that the whole affair comes to such a head that he can write of nothing else. Hewer has to be called in as an intermediary, and Pepys

L

ends at night in an unusual paroxysm of prayer and contrition and actually confesses he found no joy in looking at the hangings which the upholsterer had been putting up during the day in his "best chamber". He was really ashamed of himself at the moment. But has anyone in the world been able to write down with such precision the very good reason he had for being ashamed. On the contrary, most diarists enlarge on their contrition but conceal their fault so that a reader gives them credit for exaggerated repentance.

This was not the last unfortunate episode in their relationship, as the incident of the hot tongs prepared by Elizabeth for her husband's nose came later.

But when the Diary was closed Pepys and his wife went off for a trip in Holland and France, and no doubt enjoyed one another's company in the intervals of bickering. But within the year Elizabeth Pepys died. She received on her death a more lasting memorial than Pepys himself, for he erected a monument to her. "The sorrow and distraction" caused by his bereavement made him neglect his "private concernments", and he took no part in the election at Aldborough, where he had offered himself as candidate. Although Pepys lived for thirty-four more years he never married again.

Pepys's sister Paulina, known as Pall, threads her way through the story as a singularly unattractive figure. She is "a pretty good-bodied woman and not over thicke, as I thought she would have been, but full of freckles and not handsome in face". Samuel engaged her to come up from the country and live with him, but he made it perfectly clear that it was "not as a sister in any respect but as a servant". This was not a success, because she grew "proud and idle". "I find her", he says, "so very ill natured that I cannot love her, so cruel a hypocrite that she can cry when she pleases." His fear is, however, that if she does not marry then she "will be flung upon my hands". So he sets to work, and so do others, and five or six possible suitors for her hand are tried. But in spite of all the bargaining over her portion and their incomes nothing comes of it, and Pepys becomes alarmed, for, he remarks, "she grows old and ugly". Finally a match is made for her and she marries John Jackson in February 1667/68. Pepys is not enthusiastic: "A plain young man, handsome enough for Pall, one of no education or discourse, but of few words, and one altogether that I think will please me well enough". With a sigh of relief he hears of the marriage and writes: "So that work is, I hope, well over". Paulina became the mother of John Jackson, who was the heir to all Pepys's treasures.

Of amusing and entertaining domestic details there are no end. They are always introduced casually and in relation to the importance he attached to them at the moment. The diarist who omits trivialities which may often occupy a large part of his time and attention does so because he is thinking of someone reading his diary. He either fears to be thought petty or is reluctant to disclose the small matters which cause him irritation or pleasure. Yet human happiness is perhaps more dependent on these than on the larger concerns which appear to outsiders to illuminate or darken a man's career.

So if domestic affairs are enlarged upon it is because they are the essence of the Diary. They may constitute a detailed seventeenth-century comedy, but they also contribute to the presentation of a slice of a man's life with an actuality and realism which have never been equalled in the case of any other mortal who has ever lived.

CHAPTER IX

CONCLUSION

WE have detached Pepys the young official and tried
to look at him through the eyes of those who lived
with him. We have observed the middle-aged naval
expert as he grew in honour and as he fell from favour,
and we have dimly seen the old collector gathering
round him books and curiosities. In succeeding
generations we have discovered but scant traces of him
as he passed with the vast majority of beings into the
darkness of the forgotten past. And finally we have
rediscovered him illuminated with such brilliance as a
living being that the light which dazzles as it sparkles
on his tiniest features astounds us more even than the
man himself; all the more when we find that it is he
himself who has supplied it.

A poor, modest clerk, a rising official, a naval expert,
a wise administrator, a puritanical moralist, a devotee
of music, a patron of art, an associate of scientists and
men of letters, an author, an observer, a shrewd critic,
a loving companion, an affectionate friend, a man of
moral courage, a religious man, a ready helper, a slave
to duty, an idealist—passages from his pen can be
quoted to show he was all of these. Passages from his

pen can also be quoted to show he could be unscrupulous, cruel, sensual, greedy, drunken, untrustworthy,
false, deceitful, coarse, cowardly, childish, uneducated,
and ridiculous. The two sides may be observed in a
single day.

The right hand of the Navy indulged in sniggering
improprieties with his maids, the learned friend of
Evelyn secretly bought bawdy books, the solemn
administrator boxed his servant boys' ears and kissed
the bookseller's wife, the puritanical moralist enjoyed
obscene tales, the punctilious civil servant got drunk,
the man who braved the Plague screamed when he was
set upon by a dog, the sentimentally devoted husband
gave his wife a black eye, the man who was shocked
to see the Court playing cards on Sunday gloated
over the scandals of the King's mistresses, the connoisseur of art-treasures cut pages of manuscripts with
his scissors, the admirer of Chaucer kept Rochester's
poems in a secret drawer, the captious critic of sermons
squeezed the hand of a "pretty maid" in the pew next
him, the great librarian arranged his books according
to their size.

There is no need to go on. These may be inconsist-
encies, they are not contradictions. We must always
remember that Pepys lived in a dissolute age, in
which tolerance of vice was far more common than
appreciation of virtue. We are not dealing with the
strange phenomenon of a double personality. We
have simply got a uniquely close vision of an ordinary
human life. We are all in our way and in our time
made up like this, but we will not admit it because
we are all lacking in honesty; so we hope by reticence
and concealment that people will only notice our good

side, the side we want them to see. By pretending
to be shocked at Pepys, people are only adopting a
device to show their own superiority. We do not
mind admitting to grand faults and interesting vices.
Your Windhams, Haydons, Bashkirtseffs, Amiels,
Barbellions, even Tolstoys, may tell us of drink, debt,
profligacy, and inordinate vanity, and hint at larger
misdemeanours; but not one of them will put down in
black and white the petty, silly, mean, cowardly,
disgraceful little thoughts and actions which sully the
current pages of every human life.

Pepys managed to do it. No one else has, and it is
fairly certain that no one else will. In diaries of the
future which are not purely objective it seems likely
that psycho-analysis will only open the door to a sort
of pseudo-scientific dishonesty. Since the seventeenth
century the world has become sophisticated. With so
many literary, psychological, and scientific stores within
easy reach, raw, unsophisticated spontaneity for any
educated person becomes almost impossible.

Diaries are more than ever popular reading. Their
merit will always depend on the personality of the
writer rather than on the subjects with which he or
she deals. Personal references to living people or to
people known to those still living are eagerly read.
But very few of the productions of recent generations
have special intrinsic merit. The art of letter writing
has, owing to modern circumstances, almost vanished.
The art of diary writing is losing its natural spontaneity
and artlessness, owing to the prevalence of a desire for
publication even in the diarist's lifetime. Perhaps the
strain and bustle of modern life is inimical to the particular sort of reflective mood of self-contemplation

which leads to a natural even though secret expression of egotism.

Let publishers leave off announcing "a modern Pepys" when a new diary appears. There is going to be no modern Pepys. There may be an observer unknown and unseen among us who is noting the fashion and mood of the time, who is recording events, and criticising, satirising, or eulogising the people of our day. His method will perhaps be new, his judgements striking, but he will not give himself away, he will not be "a modern Pepys".

The Diary's vogue may vary with the taste of succeeding generations; it may be relegated to a lower or less popular position, only to be revived again in the years to come. Clouds may pass and changing taste may dim the charm of this curious book, but as long as man interests himself in life at all, it will emerge again and again as pre-eminent among all human documents, and, unlike lives of saints and records of illustrious supermen, will make its appeal to the mass of ordinary, average people.

The appeal of the Diary is indeed very wide. People of varied temperaments and occupations find pleasure in it; for to whatever class of life they may belong they will light on little reflections of themselves and little reminders of their own failings. It is not only for historians and men of letters; it is not a literary curiosity or a museum piece. It is as near a living being as any inanimate written pages can well be.

BIBLIOGRAPHY

Memoires of the Royal Navy by Samuel Pepys, 1690.
Reprinted and edited by J. R. Tanner. 1906.

Diary and Correspondence of Samuel Pepys, F.R.S. Deciphered by the Rev. J. Smith. Edited by Lord
Braybrooke. 1825; 1828; 1848–1849; 1854.

The Life Journals and Correspondence of Samuel Pepys.
Rev. J. Smith. 1841.

The Diary of Samuel Pepys. Deciphered with original notes
by the Rev. Mynors Bright. 1875–1879.

The Diary of Samuel Pepys, M.A., F.R.S. Edited by
Henry B. Wheatley, F.S.A. 8 vols. and Pepysiana.
1893.

Everyman's Library. The Diary of Samuel Pepys with a
Note by Richard Garnett, C.B. 2 vols.

Everybody's Pepys. The Diary abridged and illustrated.
Edited by O. F. Morshead. 1926.

Historical Manuscripts Commission, 15th Report, Appendix,
Part II. (Manuscript of J. Eliot Hodgkin, F.S.A.)
Pepys Papers.

A Descriptive Catalogue of the Naval Manuscripts in the
Pepysian Library. Edited by J. R. Tanner. (Navy
Records Society.) Vol. I. General Introduction. Vols.
II. and III. Admiralty Letters. Vol. IV. Admiralty
Journal. 1903–1923.

Correspondence of Samuel Pepys, 1679–1703. Edited by
J. R. Tanner. 2 vols. 1926.

Samuel Pepys's Naval Minutes. Edited by J. R. Tanner.
1926. (Navy Records Society.)

Mr. Pepys: an Introduction to the Diary together with a
Sketch of his Later Life. By J. R. Tanner. 1925.

Pepys and the World he lived in. By H. B. Wheatley. 1880.

Samuel Pepys: Lover of Music. By Sir Frederick Bridge. 1903.

Samuel Pepys: Administrator, Observer, Gossip. By E. H. Moorhouse. 1909.

Samuel Pepys. By Percy Lubbock. 1909.

The Spanish Books in the Library of Samuel Pepys. By Stephen Gaselee. 1921.

Samuel Pepys. By Gamaliel Bradford. 1925.

Samuel Pepys: a Portrait in Miniature. By J. Lucas Dubreton. 1925.

More Pepysiana. By Walter H. Whitear. 1927.

Bibliotheca Pepysiana: a Descriptive Catalogue of the Library of Samuel Pepys. I. Sea MSS. II. General Introduction and Early Printed Books. III. Mediæval MSS. 1914, 1923.

REVIEWS, ESSAYS, ARTICLES, AND LECTURES

Quarterly Review, March 1826. Review of first edition of the Diary by Sir Walter Scott.

Familiar Studies of Men and Books (Samuel Pepys). By R. L. Stevenson. 1886.

Samuel Pepys and the Royal Navy. By J. R. Tanner (Lees Knowles Lecture for 1919).

English Historical Review, April 1892. "Pepys and the Popish Plot," by J. R. Tanner.

The Atlantic Monthly, December 1890. "The Wife of Mr. Secretary Pepys," by Mrs. Margaret C. Whiting.

Medical History of Mr. and Mrs. Samuel Pepys: Why Pepys discontinued his Diary. (Papers by Sir D'Arcy Power.)

Edinburgh Review, July 1880.

Nature (by Sir Archibald Geikie), lxxi. 415.

Fortnightly Review (by Sir Sidney Lee), 1906.

Yale Review (by Wilbur C. Abbott), April 1914.

INDEX

Admiralty, the, 3, 5, 11, 23, 35, 39, 39-40, 40, 43, 47, 52, 54, 58, 81, 86, 97, 114
Admiralty Journal, 35, 97, 97 *n.*
Adventures of Five Hours, The, 128
Albemarle, Duke of, 9, 66, 100, 101
Aldborough, 146
Amiel, 82, 151
Armada, the, 34, 43
Ashmole, Elias, 53
Ashwell, Mary, 132-137

Bagwell, Mrs., 86
Baker, John (diarist), 73, 74
Barbellion, W. N. P., 82, 151
Bashkirtseff, Marie, 82, 151
Batten, Lady, 138
Beach, Sir Richard, letter to, 9
Beaumont and Fletcher, 126
"Beauty Retire" (Pepys's song), 33, 116, 119
Belasyse, Lord, letter to, 108
Betterton, Thomas, 125
Blunt, Wilfrid, 65
Bodley, Sir Thomas, 53
Boyle, Hon. Robert, 23
Braybrooke, Lord, 57, 60
Bright, Mynors (second decipherer of *Diary*), 57
Brouncker, Lord, 66, 85, 99
Burney, Fanny, 82, 97, 126
Byrom, John, 50-52, 73
Byron, 84

Cambridge, University of, 39
Carlyle, Jane Welsh, 143

Carteret, Lady, letter to, 112
Case, Mr., 92
Castle Rising, 4
Castlemaine, Lady, 16, 67, 103, 125
Catherine, Queen, 102
Cavalier (sculptor), 40
Charles II., 9, 10, 17, 22, 43, 57, 67, 80, 98, 101, 102-104, 105, 107, 110, 125, 127, 150
Charlett, Dr. Arthur, letter to, 118-119
Chaucer, 31-32, 45, 123, 150
Christ's Hospital, 30-31, 35, 45-46, 70
Clapham, 18, 23, 25, 39
Clarendon (Henry Hyde, Earl of), 27, 31, 39, 66
Clarke, Dr. and Mrs., 138-139
Clegg, Dr. James (diarist), 74-75
Clifford, Lady Anne, 69, 143
Clothworkers' Company, 35
Cocke, Captain, 20
Coleridge, on Pepys, 80-81
Committee, The, 127
Cooke, Mr., 28
Cooke, Sir Robert, 126
Cottenham, Pepys of, 6
Coventry, Sir William, 9, 46, 66, 67, 74, 86, 99, 100, 101, 102, 104, 105-108, 112, 138
Creed, John, 7
Creevey, 6
Croker, 6
Cumberland, Dr. Richard, 33-34
Cupid's Revenge, 126